SIX

Into the mountains

Our 42-seat Pakistan International Airlines flight climbed quickly with the terrain as we flew north out of Islamabad. The enormity of where we were heading—the Himalayas!— hit me as I watched the sun's rays appear and strike the world's highest mountain range. I stared, lost, nose and forehead pressed against the window. The morning exploded. The sun splashed farther peaks that were gleaming white and sharp, and then our plane was weaving through them.

I recalled E.M. Forster's desperate descriptions of the region in *A Passage to India*, that there was "something unspeakable" about these mountains, which were older than anything in the world. They rose "abruptly, insanely, without the proportion that is kept by the wildest hills elsewhere, they bear no relation to anything dreamt or seen."

I saw steep swaths of granite, snow, and tundra, and imagined walking over them. Sutay's great-grandfather had traveled here nearly a hundred years ago, and he described trips to Utror, Kalam, and Kashmir: "When we made the trip to Mt. Mankial and Ushu, the area was not considered safe and the Tehsildar sent six soldiers with us, charging a rupee a day for their services . . . Accommodations were most primitive. One night calves were turned out of their shed and we spread maple leaves on the floor and placed our bedding on the leaves. Another night we slept in a small windowless shop."

These were the Northern Areas, independent dynastic states that had become part of Pakistan only a few decades ago. Up until then, various tribes had coexisted in the sheer isolation given by these steep valleys. They still do, despite nationhood.

I was traveling deeper and farther than I ever had in my life. So transfixed was I by these thoughts and the scenery that I only awakened from the moment when sudden shouts from inside the plane pierced the drone of the turboprop engine.

My head swung around as Sutay's nails dug into my thigh. Two men were shoving each other in the aisle. Other passengers were holding them apart and shouting. Fear and adrenaline mixed with the awe I'd been feeling and I pressed Sutay to me, neither of us speaking. After the men were separated and order was restored, the air remained tense and stuffy until we landed. On the tarmac, both men were taken away by military police, who yelled at me when I snapped a photo.

It was a gorgeous morning, the sky bright blue, the air light and thin, a rainbow of wildflowers planted around the airport grounds.

This was Gilgit, the regional capital of the Northern Areas. I hurried over to Captain Khan and asked what had happened. The pilot, he explained, had given a friend prior permission to enter the cockpit but had failed to alert the undercover air marshal. When I asked about the soldiers and sandbagged bunkers around the airport in Gilgit, he said there had been sectarian violence of late.

We did not stay for the sights but headed straight to the bus lot to board a crowded minivan to Karimabad, farther still into the mountains. We packed in, Sutay and I facing each other on the benches, pressed firmly into the shoulders of our fellow travelers, mostly Hunzakuts returning home after business in Gilgit.

Our van plodded out of the lot, crossed a high bridge, and turned onto the Karakoram Highway—the KKH—the highest paved international road in the world, connecting China and Pakistan along the ancient Silk Road, right through the Karakoram and Hindu Kush ranges. At its highest point, the road crosses 15,397-foot Khunjerab Pass. More than a thousand Pakistanis and Chinese workers lost their lives during its construction, which began in 1959 and was opened to the public in 1986. Among many other important changes, the KKH opened the region up to cyclists, climbers, and mountaineers, creating a mini-boom in adventure tourism.

The people surrounding us were distinct from their countrymen to the south. Their Central Asian genes produced thick, stocky men with sun-pinked skin and squinty blue eyes. This was the only place on our entire trip where I somewhat resembled the locals. My great-grandparents were from Lithuania—at the other end of the Asian continent but close enough to grant me thick, stocky, Hunzakut street cred. Or so I liked to think.

Instead of Urdu, most people in this region spoke Burushaski, used by fewer than ninety thousand people in the world. Some claimed they were descended from soldiers in Alexander the Great's conquering Macedonian army who had passed here two thousand years ago.

The windows of the minivan were open, cool air washing in, such a relief from the temperatures in Rawalpindi and Islamabad far, far below. As we crossed a long bridge, the air cooled even more, and everyone donned the traditional flat knit wool caps, or Hunza caps.

For five hours, we ascended valleys, crossed bridges, and swerved to avoid livestock, rockslides, and lunatic oncoming buses. Sutay and I gawked at peaks above and thousand-foot drops to the river below. We teetered above raging, river-cut rocks and cliffs. The pure, ice-white peak of Mount Rakaposhi appeared every now and then up skinny valleys and then would disappear again.

The Hunza Valley is a land of steep valleys swathed in pasture and patches of poplars. Thousands of miles of stone gullies carry glacier-melt to potato patches and fruit orchards. Our vehicle climbed and twisted and climbed some more, through vast stretches of scenery and survival. As stunning as it was, it was a long day of travel, and Sutay's head slumped onto my shoulder. She slept, even as we entered Shangri-La.

Karimabad is a hill-clinging town with a single, steep, stone street lined with small shops, guesthouses, carpet stores, and chapati stands. In July 2005, Karimabad was a shell of its former existence as a world-renowned rustic mountain and trekking destination. A decade before, we were told more than once, tourists from around the world had swarmed this region in the summer. Then the events of September 11, 2001, changed the world and sparked (another) war in neighboring Afghanistan. The Hunza Valley, though peaceful, was just too close to the regional conflict for most would-be international trekkers, who no longer came to the area.

Hotels now asked a fraction of what they'd once charged. It was a bargain for us. We checked into the World Roof Hotel and received a room with the best balcony view I'd ever had in my life looking down the valley—for under $10 a night. But it was sad for a place with few alternatives to tourism to earn outside cash. During the few weeks we spent in the region, Sutay and I met the odd British or German traveler, a couple of Japanese stoners, and that was it.

The next morning the air was so cool that we couldn't wait to get out and see where we were. We began with a hike to the top of the village and then up the steps to the Baltit Fort. A museum now, the fort used to be the royal residence of the Mir, or ruler. It is a striking structure, built atop the entire steep valley and village, thrusting like the bow of a ship over it all. Sutay and I toured the fort with an ornately mustachioed gentleman guide named Ejaz, then had apricot soup and tea in a backyard café.

Dr. Stewart had visited here once. He mentioned snow leopard cubs that the Mir's children kept as pets. One of those children, Ghazanfar Ali Khan, is the present Mir of Hunza, though today, in addition to being a member of the historical royal bloodline, he is an elected official in the newly integrated system of government. He is also, we were told a few weeks before, a Gordonian, an alumnus of the school where Dr. Stewart had taught.

Since donating their ancestral home as a museum, Ghazanfar Ali Khan and his family have lived in a modern royal residence on the lower end of Karimabad, on the same property as the high-end hotel they run. The next day we took a brief tour of the hotel; it was elegant and completely empty. A few days later, when the Mir returned from business in Gilgit, we received word at our hotel from the palace that he wanted to see us in his office.

Ghazanfar Ali Khan was a serious, hair-slicked man wearing a loose cotton *shalwar kameez*. He was gracious and had a servant bring us tea and biscuits as soon as we were seated, though he did not smile once during our interview. Yes, he knew of Dr. Stewart, but the men had missed each other at Gordon College by three years. The Mir had attended the school, he told us, before President Bhutto nationalized Pakistan's mission-run schools and hospitals, condemning them to futures of mediocrity and mismanagement.

The Mir posed with us for a photo outside his office and apologized for not having more information about Dr. Stewart. Then, when I mentioned that we were planning a trip into the mountains, he gave us the name of a trekking guide, his nephew's company actually, which he promised could take care of everything.

SEVEN

Trek to Rash Peak

Rahmat Kareem kept an appropriately gear-cluttered trekking shop called Adventure Hunza just up the lane from the Roof of the World Hotel where Sutay and I had been staying for a week. It took several days of meetings before we decided on the best trek. As we planned and plotted, Sutay, Kareem, and I drank cold sodas and warm cups of milk tea while looking at maps and photos of possible routes.

I was like a kid in a candy store, browsing Himalayan valleys, camps, and glaciers—all lined up for my picking. Hiking was, after all, my thing. Ever since my mother took me on nature walks around ponds in West Virginia, I've loved to go hiking. I'd worked as an Outward Bound Wilderness instructor, U.S. Forest Service biologist, and wildland firefighter—all jobs that involved extended periods of walking in the woods

and sleeping on the ground (and getting paid overtime for it!).
I even wrote a song once called "Good Hiking."

The Himalayas—our hotel balcony looked out to the foothills of Rakaposhi—was Mecca for this hiker. I felt giddy in
Kareem's shop as we narrowed in on our routes and decided
on a weeklong loop with five glacier crossings and a summit
possibility to Rash (pronounced "rush") Peak.

Sutay, on the other hand, was not as excited about venturing
into the backcountry. She'd grown up hiking with her mother
and aunts, all of whom had inherited Dr. Stewart's predilec-
tion for walking in the mountains and bending over plants, but
she had little camping experience in such wild places. She was
also nervous about the altitude, which, if she knew anything
from growing up in the Rockies, could trigger unpredictable
altitude sickness. But because she knew how badly I wanted to
do this, she agreed to the trek.

I was torn. I didn't want to put her in danger, but I knew
that putting her—and us—through a little discomfort wasn't
necessarily a bad thing. Then again, she was my wife, not my
Outward Bound student. I wasn't sure how hard to push. In
the end, the sheer unknown of what we were signing up for
won over and we went.

On the morning of our departure, we sat on the roof of our
hotel, eating oily omelets, just as we had the previous ten morn-
ings. Our eggs came with a triangle of Laughing Cow cheese,
toast, and milk tea—eaten with a blood-rushing view down the
Hunza Valley. Then we shouldered our packs, walked to Kareem's shop, and left Karimabad in a sky-blue open-topped jeep.

Our supplies were stacked behind us in crates and blue plastic barrels. We descended one side of the valley, took a bridge over the roiling river, and climbed a series of switchbacks up the Nagar drainage on the other side.

At the end of the road, in the village of Hoper, Kareem negotiated with a waiting group of potential porters who were pleading for the work. Two men agreed to split a single man's wage, which was all Kareem was offering. Their names were Mohammed and Mohammed, an uncle and nephew. Like the others in the circle, they were dressed in worn gray *shalwar kameezes* and wool Hunza caps. The elder Mohammed had curly hair around the sides, bald on top, a mustache, and a jovial smile. The younger was dark and lean and serious. Both spoke only Burushaski. Even before the other men had dispersed, the pair were testing loads, adjusting straps, and preparing for our departure.

Our team was assembled. After cups of *doodh chai*, we were on our feet and descending to the first glacier's edge. The ice floe was enormous, more like a pile of house-sized chunks and rocks. We made our way across the dirty surface, feeling its creeks and shudders. The trail then climbed and leveled alongside another glacier, where we paused for a picnic of crackers and tinned fish.

I used the respite to find out more about our guides. Kareem was ruddy-faced and stoic. He didn't use sunscreen, just let his face burn and peel away. He grunted in response to our simple questions, short little "humphs," a habit I imitated later with Sutay, to her annoyance. Kareem had become the owner of the trekking company after several decades toiling as a porter on international alpine expeditions up some of the highest peaks in the world.

His right-hand man was Mansur, the cook. Mansur was a lean, goateed man of few words who produced delicious food, always fresh (except the canned sardines) and served on a checkered blanket spread out on the blue-iced glaciers and 15,000-foot-high yak meadows.

The elder Mohammed was in good spirits that first day, joking constantly and picking little purple flowers and giving little micro-bouquets to Sutay. During the first glacier crossing, Mohammed stopped and sang a song in Burushaski, which Kareem told us was a love song. When I asked what it meant, he said, "Humph! It is too sad to translate."

———————

Day two was grueling, as we hiked to the top of the ridge that hemmed in the double-glacier valley. The steep trail had few switchbacks and no trees. Sutay began in decent spirits, though I could tell she was nervous. I tried to talk to her as we climbed, but we were both too out of breath. I watched her mood darken as the vertical feet continued and soreness and shortness of breath blanketed every step. She wasn't defeated, she was simmering, even amid all this beauty. After all, the trek had been *my* idea. *I* was the reason she was suffering right now.

I felt guilty, but knew this would pass and we'd be on top and she'd be happy for it. Isn't challenging each other part of what marriage is about? Wouldn't I also want to be pushed into something new? Maybe not, I guess, if it meant pain and not being able to breathe. We climbed past 14,000 feet above sea level and the scale of the scenery grew with every step.

We ate lunch with a 360-degree view of the high Himalayas. We sat on our checkered picnic blanket and looked at the alpine world through our sunglasses. The break distracted Sutay from her struggles; I saw her lighten and laugh when Mohammed gave her another tiny bouquet. Her cheeks were rosy with the exertion and sun, and the food helped us both. As we rested, I photographed butting yaks, merging glaciers, and Mansur's triumphant silhouette against backdrops of icy peaks.

We walked through the afternoon and made camp in a high meadow facing the longest alpine panorama I have ever seen. After sunset, tiny specks of orange appeared far, far below. "You can see the fires," said Kareem. Flecks of light were multiplying as we watched. "They are dancing and singing and making the fires. Today is July 11, the birthday of the Aga Khan's reign. We are celebrating."

Like most of the population in this area, Kareem, Mansur, and both Mohammeds are Ismaili Muslims, a Shi'ah sect whose devotees live in pockets across the world and follow the teaching of the Aga Khan, an imam based in France. The Aga Khan also runs an international development organization responsible for a vast network of health, environmental, and micro-finance projects in the Hunza Valley and beyond. The current Aga Khan encourages his followers to learn English and become citizens of the world. On his website he emphasizes "the view of Islam as a thinking, spiritual faith: one that teaches compassion and tolerance and that upholds the dignity of man, Allah's noblest creation."

The sunset had carried on for hours and our dinner of curry and rice was warm in our bellies as darkness descended and the fires shone below. Cradling cups of tea brewed from a flower that the Mohammeds had collected along the trail, Sutay and I stood on the mountain with our companions around our own tiny fire.

Suddenly, Mohammed the elder jumped up, yelped, and hooked his nephew's elbow in his, as the two began singing and clapping. Sutay and I joined in, swinging partners like in a square dance, the lights below, Kareem and the porters clapping and chanting.

When the effort and altitude and the effects of the day's work hit us like a wall, we retired to our tent. Everyone stopped dancing after we left, but we could hear them murmuring quietly by the fire as we fell asleep.

I awoke at first light, Sutay sleeping next to me on the earth, lifelong dreams of mine colliding with hers as I watched the soft curves on her breathing face. I kissed her cheek, then zipped open the world and emerged into it.

After breakfast, we split up so I could bag Rash Peak. Sutay seemed to be doing fine where we'd camped, but that day's route would require her to cross a 15,000-foot pass skirting the frozen shore of Rash Lake. I left her in the hands of Mansur and the porters and took off with Kareem up an iced-over ridge to a stone pile at 16,500 feet—Rash Peak, the highest I'd ever climbed.

At the summit, a brief moment of good weather allowed me to strip down to a T-shirt, which whipped in thin-aired winds. K2 and other famous peaks remained obscured by distant clouds, but I didn't care. I grew light-headed as I descended, experiencing moments of numbness as I hopped from rock to rock, as if I was not touching the ground. I can't believe I didn't fall and break an ankle.

Meanwhile, below, Sutay was feeling weaker and finding it even harder to breathe. The guides were concerned when she clutched at her throat and slowed to a crawl. They made it across the pass and were able to descend a few hundred feet, where she improved, while they waited for Kareem and me in a cold drizzle. Reunited, we began a steep, monotonous descent to our next camp at the foot of the glacier.

Six hours later the day was coming to an end. Kareem stayed with us as we struggled, weary of steep and slick trails, while Mansur and the Mohammeds bounded down the hill to make camp and start dinner. The glacier's gray-stained edge rose in a sixty-foot tower above the red specks of our tents, still far below.

Kareem stopped suddenly and bellowed down the hill, his voice crossing an impossible distance down the slope. I didn't think the others would hear him, but then I saw them, like ants below, wave in reply.

"What did you say to them?" I asked.

"I told Mohammed to bring tea for Madame," he answered.

I thought he was joking; there's no way he would make anyone climb back up that hill when we would be down in less than an hour. But that's what he did. Both Mohammeds made the trip. Soon we were sipping hot, fresh-plucked Hunza tea from a thermos while the porters barreled back down.

We spent the final night of our trek at a summer encampment of goatherds from Hoper village. The goat camp was barren, not a single tree but many rocks, most of which had been used to construct a system of walls, paths, and structures. The rocks formed wells, irrigation ditches, storage facilities, and homes. There was even a small stone mosque, open on one side and carpeted with goat skins.

"You must buy a ram," explained Kareem as we walked into the camp. It was news to me but I didn't argue. "Baksheesh," he clarified. I gave him the cash.

When I was introduced to the elder of the camp, I found that, lo and behold, I had bought a ram. We watched them kill and slaughter it amid the stark stone scenery, then Sutay and I retreated to our tent, pitched in a field grazed to a putting green by the animals.

Our perch overlooked the two glaciers we'd crossed that morning. We could see them clearly as they each descended from a different high crease in the rocks, each with a different color and texture as they merged. The grays, blues, and whites of the ice floes started side-by-side, then churned together and continued downslope as one.

When the food was ready, a boy brought a tin plate to our tent door. On it was the goat's liver sprinkled with precious salt and fried in oil. Sutay demurred, so I carried the plate to share with Kareem and Mansur. The three of us squatted, breaking off bits of liver with our right hands.

It took a few hours longer for the rest of the meat to be ready. While we waited for it to cook, I played tug-of-war with the teenage boys, me versus four or five of them. The men stood around in their wool caps and cotton *kameezes*. I wore the tan *shalwar kameez* I'd bought in Rawalpindi. The boys pulled me across green skids of turf. When dinner was ready, Sutay had a few polite, gristly bites of ram meat and I ate till I couldn't any more. As it grew dark and cool, the stars came out.

The next morning, after a prolonged breakfast, we said good-bye to our hosts. I'm sure we weren't the only foreigners Kareem had ever hauled through that camp, but I'm also sure there were not many who came that year. The goatherds lined up shoulder to shoulder, waving and watching as we walked away and rounded a fold of land. Then they were gone in the mist.

It had been a fortifying, burly trek, and now it was all downhill. The final day's hike was long, gray, quiet, drizzly, and thoughtful. The image of ice rivers flowing into each other and becoming one stayed in my mind as I watched Sutay move through the mist in front of me, a far more confident creature than the one who had been struggling a few days before. What else would happen as we continued to mix like the glaciers under our feet?

We savored our return to "civilization" in Karimabad, not knowing that a power outage would mean candle-lit, freezing-cold bucket baths instead of the hot showers we'd been anticipating for a week. Kareem wanted to take us on another trek—to Rakaposhi base camp. Knowing full well we may never be back here again in our lives, I was so tempted, but we declined. It was time to head east to our volunteer assignment awaiting us in India. Before we left for the capital, we sipped a final cup of tea with Kareem, sitting at his desk, skin peeling from his cheeks, surrounded by backpacks and ice axes. We thanked him and said goodbye.

"Humph," he growled, smiling broadly and shaking my hand in a rock-like grip.

EIGHT

Near miss

Fearful of stranding ourselves in Gilgit, which although beautiful, was a bit too militarized for our taste, and knowing that the flight to Islamabad was often canceled due to inclement weather, Sutay and I chose our only other option to leave the Hunza Valley (besides traveling in the opposite direction, illegally, into China, that is): an overnight NatCo bus trip from Aliabad down the Karakoram Highway.

This route goes through the notorious Indus Kohistan and Swat Valley regions, which our guidebook called "pretty lawless." We were advised not to travel at night *anywhere* on the Karakorum Highway. This wasn't possible, however, since our only option down was the 27-hour NatCo ride. Not knowing what else we could do, we got on the bus.

We were the only foreigners on the bus and Sutay was the only female. The ride was as physically uncomfortable as the scenario was sketchy. Because our seats were above the rear wheels, we felt every bump and hole on the road. Plus, from our raised vantage point, we watched the bus swing wildly with every turn so that as the most stunning scenery in the world passed outside our windows, we saw only a swervy tunnel of near-nausea.

Breathe in through the nose, taste the saliva in the mouth, survive one turn, one bump at a time. It was going to be a long ride.

We survived the first part of the journey pretty well, turning back and forth, getting used to the motion, and as night fell, dozing off and on. At a middle-of-the-night bathroom break and dahl stop next to a roaring waterfall, I left Sutay sleeping in the bus. I was famished and the driver assured me she would be okay. I trusted him. As I exited, he said, "We wait for another bus."

"Why?" I asked.

"To travel together," he said. "Safer. Because of fundamentalists. And in case of rock fall—more people to dig."

I joined a group of men from our bus for a midnight meal. I followed their lead and splashed bracing stream water on my face to clean off the dust. Then we climbed atop a kind of rope bed and sat cross-legged, dipping chapatis into tin plates of lentils. A boy poured *doodh chai* into small glasses.

A man from the bus introduced himself to me as Khalid and he paid for my meal and showed me how to eat it—my fumbling fingers producing much laughter, relieving some of the tension from the exhausting ride.

I took Sutay a few toasty chapatis, which she nibbled as the bus started back up. Our convoy of three vehicles pulled onto the highway and I fell into a torturous head-bobbing nonsleep.

My nap was interrupted suddenly by shouting in the darkness. The bus had stopped. Before I'd quite awoken, I was being led up the aisle and outside into the rain to stand next to a canvas military tent. Low-slung Kalashnikovs bumped against my legs as passports bounced from my trembling hands into the mud. As I bent to retrieve them, Khalid arrived out of nowhere. He had a flashlight and was speaking to the soldiers and pulling me up by the arm.

This was the first and only checkpoint we encountered in Pakistan. At the time, I had no idea if it was common. I still don't. But I passed and was back on the bus before the adrenaline kicked in. Then we were traveling again, and I was wide awake. I sat with Khalid in the back of the bus, talking quietly to while away the pre-dawn grayness.

He was a scientist, he said, from Rawalpindi. He spoke in a high, hoarse voice. He had been trekking with friends in the mountains and had lost his voice arguing with them. They had argued so much that he'd stormed off to catch a bus by himself rather than fly with them from Gilgit.

"I also went to Gordon College!" he squeaked when I told him of our mission. "I have a photograph of Madame's ancestor at my home," he said, nodding toward Sutay who slept at my side, and referring to her great grandfather, Dr. Stewart.

We were nearly down. Only a few hours left and the motion would stop. Pastel light filled the sky, more and more of which was visible as we emerged from the final, steep canyon. Before the sun was up, the driver pulled over to a small stone mosque for morning prayers; everyone filed out while Sutay and I wandered in the opposite direction, stretching and rubbing our faces. In the strange silence, I pressed her back to my chest and we both watched the sky. After fifteen minutes or so, we rejoined the men back on the bus and kept riding.

———————

Khalid and I resumed our discussion as Sutay curled up to go back to sleep in our seat. He asked permission to read my palm and cradled my hand in his. We sat sideways, hunched together across the aisle.

"You have a sharp mind, robust health, and much energy, especially for your work," Khalid said. "Still, you need a guide." He gestured to Sutay. "If Madame is a good guide and a good friend, you will go far."

I nodded. She was. We would.

He pored over my mystery cross, a crease in the center of the palm between the head and heart lines, then my life line. The other men on the bus slept or watched us through scruffy faces wrapped in wool scarves and head wraps. Droning devotional music played on scratchy, jury-rigged speakers as the sky grew lighter. Through the windows, racing green foothills had replaced sheer gray cliffs and canyons.

"What is he singing?" I asked, pointing to the speakers.

"This is Nusrat Fateh Ali Khan," said Khalid. "He is singing, 'To love is not easy; it is a river of fire and we swim in it.'"

———————

We lingered a few days in the capital, then boarded an air-conditioned express bus to Lahore, en route to the border with India. This trip was worlds away from the NatCo bus nightmare from Aliabad, luxurious in comparison. We looked out the wide windows, and an attendant came down the aisle to pour tea and pass out newspapers.

I opened my paper to a one-column, spine-chilling article about a NatCo bus that had just been ambushed on the Karakoram Highway—the day before. The attacked bus had departed 24 hours after ours, driven the same route, and was shot at by "religious extremists" in a narrow canyon. Eight had been killed, including the driver. I showed it to Sutay and we said nothing, just let it slip away as we sped east across the plains to Lahore.

NINE

Sufi night

We found the entrance to the Regale Internet Inn, a hostel just off the Regal Chowk, between a lopsided tea cart and a man squatting and sipping a tiny cup. *"Feel at ease"* said the tiny sign amidst a jumble of wires above the door.

I paid our driver, then we squeezed with our packs up three narrow flights of stairs to a cluttered office where a young man at the desk greeted us with a "salaam."

"How many nights?" he asked as he handed me a padlock and key.

"Just one," I said.

I was sure of this. The worst heat wave in a century was smothering Lahore with temperatures well over a hundred degrees Fahrenheit. The polluted air stung our eyes as we rode

across town to the hotel. No, we had no intention of exploring.
We were too fixed on getting to India to give Lahore its due.

Yet there we were, in one of the great cities of the East—
the Heart of Pakistan, Garden of the Mughals, the Prince of
the Punjab! Founded four thousand years ago by Lav, son of
Rama, Lahore was now about to be dismissed by two clueless
American tourists as an annoying stopover. In that exhausted
moment of arrival, we just didn't care. After several days of un-
settling travel from Hunza and Islamabad, we were just happy
to stop, even for just a night.

Inside the inn, a small, international youth hostel, shirtless,
hungry-looking travelers buzzed in all directions—scuttling
through twisted hallways and shared spaces, clinking around
the outdoor kitchen: cups of tea, open backpacks, laundry drying. The social activity was heartening, but the condition of
our room was not. It was barely bigger than the sagging, clap-
board bed touching three of the four cardboard walls. There
was one lazy ceiling fan and no other furniture.

We put our things down and went back outside. On the
rooftop, a ladder led to a ten-foot-square, broken-brick, fly-
ridden lounge area where a few sheets of tin provided some
shade as a weak breeze blew through. The few fellow guests
sitting there welcomed us with smiles and indications of where
to sit.

I leaned against the crumbling wall. For the first time in
days, I was able to relax. The filthy plastic mat covering the
concrete felt like a deep couch cushion as I dropped into it, and
Sutay did the same.

"This is called the 'tribal area,'" said a smiling 19-year-old.
He reached out his hand. "I am Ciro, from Venezuela."

"Why is it called the tribal area?" I asked.

"Because there are no laws here," he said. Ciro grinned and squatted, barefoot in a small mountain of cigarette butts, matches, rolling papers, and dust. We began the familiar backpacker ritual, the sizing up: How long have you been traveling? Where are you from? Where have you been? Where are you headed?

Sutay and I were on an extended honeymoon, we told him. We'd arrived that day by bus. We were on our way to a volunteer assignment north of Calcutta, India. Our site was clear across the subcontinent in West Bengal, and we had one month to report for duty.

Ciro nodded his approval. He was westbound after six months in India; he was traversing Pakistan, Iran, and Turkey. "I will take the Orient Express when I get to Turkey!" he said. He would eventually return to Paris to school.

His excitement was unbridled. This was Ciro's first big trip, and he was floating on the freedom of it, happy to be introducing us to the scene, inducting us into the tribe, sitting on a rooftop in Lahore, standing suddenly to watch a flock of pigeons fly against the setting sun.

The bricks behind my back were still warm, but the cooler temperature brought on by the evening was lifting everyone's moods. There was more talking, laughter. I sat and scrawled in a soggy notebook as more strangers arrived, each face popping up the ladder with a smile. Monika was a solo Australian who'd just shaved her head. She sat next to Sutay. Then a lanky Latino appeared and Ciro introduced him as "El Boliviano."

"El Boliviano came to Lahore to learn the harmonium," said Ciro.

El Boliviano smiled and sat. He'd been staying in the Regale Internet Inn for three months, he said. He was studying *qawwali,* a type of music used by Sufi Muslims to meditate and induce a "nearness to God."

I reveled in the growing camaraderie, in our respective missions. Some hotels isolate their guests, keeping them apart; others bring strangers together by virtue of the common space. The tribal area accomplished the latter magnificently.

"This week, Sufi night is on the full moon!" Ciro said, rocking back and forth. "Gonga and Mithu will be drumming *dhol!*"

"They are brothers," said El Boliviano. He took a CD from his worn leather man-satchel. The cover was a blurred shot of the musicians spinning in circles as they drummed.

"What is 'Sufi night'?" I asked.

"Every Thursday night," El Boliviano began, "for the last five hundred years in Lahore, there is a tribute at the tomb of Baba Shah Jamal, a Sufi saint."

I read the CD case in my hand. It said the rhythms of *dhol* are used to catalyze the mind of the devotee as he is seeking a spiritual trance.

Recognizing and accepting new travel suggestions is not always easy or obvious, especially when you think you already have a plan. But on this evening, things could not have been clearer or more enticing. Full moon. Spiritual trance. Sufi night. My traveler's radar bristled with the possibilities.

"Malik arranges everything," Ciro said, still talking about Sufi night. "He is the hotel owner, Malik Karammat Shams."

I looked at my wife, a few feet away across the circle, sunglasses and scarf clamped on top of her head, nodding as Monika spoke to her. She looked up from her new friend and met my eyes across the tribal area. Thursday was three days away. We had planned to be in the mountains in India by then, out of this horrid heat.

Sutay and I have always shared a rare synchronicity—finishing each other's sentences, predicting each other's desires. Traveling gave us a whole new realm in which to connect in this way. That's how in that instant, without speaking a word, I knew we would stay.

TEN

Tour de Lahore

My wife's palm sweat mixed with mine as we held hands in the back of an auto-rickshaw in Lahore. It wasn't just the heat. Rickety trucks, buses, and smoke-spewing cars swarmed us on all sides. It was a little nerve wracking.

Malik Karammat Shams, our guesthouse owner, sat across from us, staring thoughtfully at the traffic. In the alley outside the Regale Internet Inn, Malik had given our driver directions to the Data Ganj Bakhsh Hajveri, a mosque and shrine. He organized our group—about a dozen foreign travelers—with a flurry of whistling, pointing, and shouting until we were loaded up. Malik climbed in with us and relaxed during the ride, until his next task as tour guide was called for. Our little rickshaw gang revved up and entered the ridiculous traffic, driving in formation toward our goal.

A retired journalist, Malik had taken over a small hostel in order to get out of the rat race and meet interesting people, he told me. He wore a loose, blue cotton outfit; he was comfortable in his role as guide, host, and wise uncle. He smoked cigarettes with a lean, concentrated look on his face as he planned the logistics of the day's trip.

When we arrived at the shrine, Malik led us down marble stairs to a wide basement room filled with hundreds of men sitting on the tile floor. He led us to the front row, where we sat down, all of us wearing thin *shalwar kameezes*, Monika and Sutay wearing headscarves. (Malik kept a stash of appropriate clothing in his hotel for unprepared guests.)

Eight musicians sat crossed-legged on the stage, microphones pointing to bearded mouths and singing instruments, the music in full swing. This was *qawwali*, a devotional droning mantra sung over tablas and harmoniums. Most of the audience sat, listened, swayed, and meditated, while a few men danced and spun in the open space before us, and others stepped forward to shower the musicians with money, dropping rupee notes over their heads.

Malik charged no money for his part of the cultural tours, only enough to cover transport, food, and water. His trips were carefully planned but carried an edge. He seemed to enjoy intentionally pushing the boundaries of where tourists were seen and tolerated in Pakistan. Perhaps he was trying to educate his countrymen as much as his guests. "I want people to experience the reality of Pakistani culture," he said. "I want to show you Pakistan. I feel that I am Pakistan, so I want to show you myself."

The next morning, we again gathered in the alley outside the hotel with our fellow hostel guests. We were a ragtag group from Argentina, Israel, Australia, Korea, Germany, Japan, and the U.S. Sutay and I were the token North Americans. We all crushed into a dilapidated van, each of us grasping a water bottle, scarf, and day pack. The van took us out of the city and into the countryside, to the village of Jandiala Sher Khan.

A country fair of sorts was going on, Malik told us, a mischievous grin on his face. "Ninety-five percent of the inhabitants of Jandiala Sher Khan have never seen a foreigner," he said as we unloaded, not giving us much time to digest this information.

The festival organizer and chief of police greeted us, then paraded us through the grounds. Our security force now included several armed officers and soldiers, plus Malik's normal entourage from the hotel. Television crews asked us for interviews as we were swept along, and people pointed and laughed at the out-of-place *Angrezis*.

The fairgrounds had somewhat familiar-looking game booths, rides, and food stands, but there were also a few anomalies, chief of these a stage full of cross-dressing men singing karaoke next to a ring-of-death motocross track. Daredevil drivers ran motorcycles and beater cars up on the boards while we stood on the rickety walkway above, looking down on them and listening to the music from the transvestite stage.

We walked to a playing field to watch a team-wrestling tournament between soldiers, possibly Army vs. Navy. We sat at the edge of the fray, swirls of shiny-dusty men, with drums beating in afternoon light.

When the sun went down, Malik led us through a muddy-lane bazaar into someone's home. There, we were honored guests—an unwashed knot of nomads serving as ambassadors from around the world. We piled into our host's bedroom where we took off our shoes and lounged on the family bed surrounded by staring women and children. A few of the kids giggled as we sat in uncomfortable silence. The sky turned dusky orange, and we were led up a series of bamboo ladders to a flat, open-air rooftop.

Fifteen of us sprawled on cane mats, drank *doodh chai*, passed hash-and-tobacco cigarettes, and looked around at the festival, fireworks, and small sea of roofs. As a dust storm threatened, we cowered on our stomachs. When the storm brought rain and gusts of cooled air, we retreated downstairs and sat in circles on the floor in someone's bedroom in candlelight.

The power was out in the whole village and we waited for dinner. It was not so uncomfortable now. Someone brought the food, hot chapatis and the best dahl any of us had ever tasted. We scooped it up with the bread amid laughter, talking, and gallons of tea. Then we thanked our hosts and left for the long, cramped ride back to Lahore.

———

That was how we passed our days at the Regale Internet Inn— going on a series of unthinkable day trips, hanging out in the rooftop "tribal area," and waiting for Thursday: Sufi night.

"Are you going to Sufi night? Who's going to Sufi night?"

The question floated around the hostel's kitchen and tribal area all week. The Regale community's week revolved around Thursday, which finally arrived. Once again, we gathered in the alley. Only this time, it was already dark, and we had a long night ahead.

Dhol, Malik explained that night as we waited for the auto-rickshaws to arrive, was similar to *qawwali*. It helped musicians and listeners establish a "nearness to God." Every Thursday at midnight in Lahore for the past five centuries, followers honored the saint Baba Shah Jamal with a *dhol* drumming session at his tomb. On this night, a full moon made it extra auspicious, and we would be there.

We rickshawed across the city, unloaded, then followed Malik through orange darkness and a thick crowd. As we approached the entrance, we passed a group of women who were only allowed to watch the drumming from behind a chain link fence. We didn't have time to ponder this as we were pushed forward, then seated in the inner circle of musicians.

The access Malik granted us to his city and people was so incredible that I questioned whether we should even be there, whether we were seeing too much. That doubt disappeared as we were welcomed like old friends. Men smiled and made room for us, clapping us on the back as we settled on the ground. Hash-laced cigarettes floated from hand to hand, mouth to mouth, smoke spreading under the branches of the squat tree that rose from the saint's tomb. The moon appeared behind the tree, and the brothers Gonga and Mithu Sain stood up and began testing their drums to the roars of the crowd. They were enormous men, curly-locked giants. They rooted their feet to their spots and stood shoulder to shoulder. Then they began beating both ends of their heavy, low-slung drums. They tuned and tightened, then synched and the music took off.

Sutay and I remained cross-legged, surrounded by men in every direction. We were at the pulsing center of it, the thump and chaos of the drums, our legs burning from sit-squatting on the concrete, the blue-smoky crowd pressing, flies, dirt,

warmth, and the taking-in-of-us, smiles between me and musicians, between me and my wife.

After several hours, the air became crisp and charged. It was
late. We realized the brothers had just been warming up and
the show had barely begun. It was a hard realization as fatigue
set in, yet we wanted to milk every moment we could of this
rare opportunity. Still, Malik had already gone. So had most
of our group.

Sutay, Ciro the Venezuelan, and I were the only *Angrezis*
left. The air was close, stuffed, and dense, sweat streaming and
flying from the drummers' heads, drums taut, sharp, rolling,
rolling, three hours, four hours, five hours, then a wall of exhaustion, and we had to push through the crowd to escape,
pushing even when errant hands reached out at Sutay's body—
assaulted again in Pakistan and there was nothing I could do
but push her through the crowd!—until finally, we made it to
the Regale Internet Inn and into our flimsy cube of a room.

We were charged and tired from the night and disgusted
from the final, yucky minutes after such an amazing scene.
Our emotions mixed with everything else and we rinsed off
with splashes of water in the shared "shower," which was more
of a drippy faucet. Even after bathing, we remained coated
with the film of the night, shiny like the full moon, sooty like
the rickshaw exhaust, danced-up dust, the danger, sweat-dried-
more-sweat. These new layers, more than memory, formed a
skin over our bodies, the core, the root, the reason we'd left in
the first place.

Sufi night summed it up neatly—the risk and reward, the
rarest of moments.

PART II

INDIA

ELEVEN

The border at Wagah

The taxi from Lahore dropped us near a used bookseller, where we stood and checked our money belts, straps, and zippers one last time. I looked at Sutay, her face tense around her sunglasses, all business and no smiles as we walked into the no-man's-land between two countries. We would enter India by foot at Wagah, located on the Grand Trunk Road between Lahore and Amritsar, and the only road border crossing between Pakistan and India. Wagah is an enormous border, famous for its flag-lowering ceremony, a daily show in which outrageously bedecked border guards from both countries tried to out-pomp each other in their marching exercises. The performance is supposed to be a loud, colorful, and healthy alternative to violence between two countries frequently at each other's throats, and it is a local must-see tourist attraction.

We were crossing too early in the morning to catch the show, but we didn't care. We were concerned only with making it to the other side with no problems. Sutay despised all airport security and border crossings, and I knew she was not alone; those things are about as popular as paper cuts. Part of it was the general anxiety everyone has at these places, but part of it had to do with her name change.

Before we'd left, Sutay had used our marriage as an opportunity to legally take the adopted African name she'd been given during her time in The Gambia, in addition to taking my last name. She'd been using "Sutay" since her Peace Corps service a decade earlier. We had assumed the National Passport Center would have given her a brand-new document for her brand-new name. But only a few weeks before our departure, they returned her old passport with an amateur-looking dot-matrix addendum printed on the inside back cover. Her passport name was now completely different from the one on her airplane tickets and visas. So far, it hadn't been a problem, but this was our first border crossing by land. It was a honeymoon hazard we hadn't anticipated.

As we began our hike across the border, an insane sun pounded down and we turned briefly to watch a group of Indian peaceniks pile out of a bus and start waving flags, banging drums, and shouting through megaphones to demand openness between the two countries. Public transport between India and Pakistan had only recently resumed. We passed the activists and entered the gauntlet.

"You smoke?" said the first border guard, looking up from our passports and putting his fingers to his lips in the universal joint-smoking sign. "Hashish?" he clarified.

"No, sir," I said.

"Document fee."

Of course. How much, sir? We had no idea what it should be, our guidebook didn't say, but we paid it. A pair of escorts arrived to accompany us to the next post, beginning a bizarre process in which teams of baggage handlers and officials passed us off to each other, with brief chatter that I'm sure meant, "These *Angrezis* will pay whatever you ask."

Which we did.

Hundred-rupee notes flowed as freely as our sweat as we advanced from station to station, showing our passports each time and wondering who would bring up Sutay's name change. Nobody did. We walked across long fortified stretches of asphalt, through massive gateways and fences, and finally between the empty parade stands where the flag ceremony would be held that evening. We started to relax, until we re-membered where we were headed. After all, we'd been warned about India.

"India—very dirty!" a traveler named Kazu in Pakistan had cautioned, shaking his head and cringing to think about it.

"Very very dirty!" his friend Hiro had confirmed.

Kazu and Hiro were a Japanese Cheech-and-Chong duo vacationing in Karimabad, the trekking base in Pakistan's Northern Areas. We had met them in our hotel there when they came stumbling out of their room across from ours, Jeff Spicoli-style, in a cloud of smoke. They had traveled to Paki-stan in search of a famed strand of hash they said was called "Peshawar Number One." In fact, the phrase "Peshawar Num-ber One" was the only English they knew (besides "very dirty," that is).

The first night we had hung out, we drank milk tea with them on the hotel's roof, under the stars, trying—and mostly failing—to breach the language barrier. Kazu and Hiro resorted to acting out parts of their horrific journey through Delhi and all the dirty things they'd seen in India, but usually just broke into head-shaking laughter and lit another joint.

Other, more serious warnings I'd heard about India flashed through my mind, like Rodger Kamenetz's descriptions in *The Jew and the Lotus* of "the total density of suffering, the immense need of the people, the vibrant anarchy of their lives." He'd observed "beggars waited at every corner, each demanding attention and care impossible to give in such quantity." This is the kind of thing I'd heard about, this is what I expected. Vibrant, depressing anarchy. Everywhere. But I'd heard about India's other side as well, the beauty, the scale of it, the mysticism. Such was the subcontinent's allure—powerful, scary, seductive. And it was a hundred feet away and getting closer with every step.

By the time Sutay and I emerged from the last little office where we finally received our Indian entry stamps, I steeled myself for what we'd encounter—even a boiling sea of aggressive touts and limbless lepers, pushing at us from piles of excrement.

When I saw what was actually there beyond the final set of gates, I softened and breathed deeply. A loose handful of Sikh men lounged under the shade of a tree, waiting for us to approach. It was peaceful and anticlimactic. The men politely answered our questions about traveling to Amritsar, less than an hour away, and then offered to sell us cold beers and taxi service to the city. After Pakistan, "the land of the pure" and dry (the only place we found alcohol was in a backyard party of expats living in Islamabad), we gladly bought two liter-sized sweaty-cold bottles of Indian beer and enjoyed them thoroughly before we got into the car.

Our anxiety shifted immediately, and not because of the quick, fizzy beer buzz. I could see it in Sutay's posture as she relaxed in the seat and leaned her elbow on the open window. Pakistan had been hard, even traumatic, for her. Though she'd felt safe and comfortable in the mountains, things had been different in Islamabad and Rawalpindi. In those cities, men had leered at her, even touched her. She'd felt angry stares from some women, too, even though she took great care to cover up and dress respectfully. We never figured it out, but on this day, I could see that she was eager to move on.

Coming off the edginess of the border crossing, India was a haven—and we hadn't even been there an hour. Sutay looked at me and we had another of our telepathic moments, this one of pure peace and relief. In Amritsar, we found a hotel by the train station and ordered sandwiches and more beer to the room. We bathed, collapsed onto the bed, then made love and napped the afternoon away. When we awoke, we pulled ourselves together for a sunset visit to the Golden Temple.

Sikhs are followers of Guru Nanak Dev, a philosopher-saint who sat and meditated on the site of the Golden Temple five hundred years ago, when the spot contained nothing more than a small lake surrounded by forest. The lake has since been enlarged and enshrined, and Guru Dev's adherents—Sikhs—make up the world's fifth-largest organized religion. We took a bicycle rickshaw to the entrance, then crossed the wide plaza, took our shoes off, and went inside.

The gilded temple forms an island in the middle of the water and is connected to the surrounding bright-white buildings by a long, narrow causeway. When we arrived, the place was crowded with a slowly moving line of people making their way around the water and toward the central shrine, some stopping to bathe. We watched people bob in the sacred water, in gilded light, ripples and reflections of gold, as chanting and tabla music from inside the shrine was broadcast on tinny speakers and wafted across the water.

The whole atmosphere stood in stark contrast to how we'd felt on the clogged, polluted streets of Lahore, from where we'd just come. It was also another reminder of the glaring misperceptions I'd held about India's presumed mayhem. Our soft landing in India extended with the long sunset, the night, and the train to catch in the morning.

TWELVE

Woodstock

We had five weeks to traverse the Indian subcontinent and report for our volunteer assignment in Calcutta. We traveled this distance of nearly 2000 miles from Pakistan to West Bengal almost entirely in trains and buses along the Grand Trunk Road, one of the oldest and longest roads in Asia. Along the way, we took side trips to Indian hill stations, higher-altitude colonial-tinged towns which provided relief from the heat and also part of our mission to track down Sutay's family legacy.

We'd begun our trip in Islamabad, looking up her great-grandfather Dr. Stewart's connections in Rawalpindi and following some of his forays into the mountains. Now we were traveling the same route that he and his wife must have taken to visit their two daughters attending the Woodstock School in Mussoorie.

We visited Dharamsala first, the misty mountain home of the Dalai Lama and multitudes of Tibetan refugees. From there, a sleepless, neck-wringing overnight bus delivered us to Dehra Dun at dawn. In a thick, gray drizzle, a classy, smooth-cornered white Ambassador taxi pulled up and we got in. The road twisted up toward Mussoorie, a dripping wet, green-mossy hill town, only a few hours north of Delhi and the site of numerous boarding schools still.

"Jamma," as all the grandchildren called her, had played an exotic presence throughout my wife's childhood. Born and raised in India (actually, born in Jhelum, Pakistan, pre-partition), the daughter of American botanist Dr. Ralph Randles Stewart, Jamma had kept an anteater as a pet in India. She'd eaten grasshoppers. She spoke strange languages called Hindi and Urdu. Sutay and her cousins knew these details.

"She was different from other grandmas," Sutay said. As a child, Sutay never fully understood why or how she was different, only that she wasn't as warm, cuddly, and doting as her friends' grandparents. "She didn't bake us cookies," she said.

It wasn't until Sutay traveled to Africa at the age of 24 and experienced a taste of life abroad that she gained some insight into her grandmother's peculiarities. But by the time she returned, Jamma had passed away.

It was then that Sutay decided somewhere in the back of her mind to go to India and see for herself the places where Jamma had grown up. She didn't necessarily know exactly *how* visiting India would help her better understand her grandmother, or *what*, if anything, it would change, but she sensed that it was an important trip to take. Some day.

As the Ambassador continued up the hill, we began passing people dressed in orange, walking or cycling along the sides of the road. They carried orange flags and trident spears. It was a *yatri*, our driver said, a religious pilgrimage in honor of Shiva.

These pilgrims travel with a purpose: to honor a certain deity in a certain place at a certain time of year. We would see them around northern India on their various missions, always dressed in orange or white. We joined them in Mussoorie, where we discovered that the pilgrims had taken all the cheap hotels in town. We settled for an overpriced, moldy affair that looked like the setting for a Bollywood horror movie. After checking in and drying off, we were looking out the window when, out of the fog, a black-faced monkey with dewy hair appeared on our balcony. I jumped. The monkey jumped and perched on the railing. She had wild eyes, a fierce mane of hair, and a baby clinging to her belly. I snapped a photo before she leapt back into the whiteness.

That afternoon, we joined the shopping, strolling throngs on Mussoorie's main drag. The pedestrian street that ran along the spine of this small mountain ridge was clogged with crowds of both *yatri* pilgrims and Indian tourists from Delhi. Families and honeymooners mixed loudly with uniformed students, everyone shopping in the trinket stalls and strutting down the lane. Sutay and I stopped at a sweets shop for a silver plate of hot *gulab jamun*, deep-fried milk balls drenched in rose syrup.

Now eighty years after Ellen Stewart and her sister, Jean, had attended school here, Mussoorie was still kind of a hub for exclusive, international private schools. The Woodstock School was built in 1854 to provide "a Protestant education for girls"; it was one of the most prestigious places for Dr. Stewart to send his children while he pressed his plants and ran his school in Rawalpindi.

After graduating from Woodstock, Ellen had made her first trip to the United States at the age of 18. She went to college in New York where she met her husband, "Dado," a cartographer for the U.S. Geological Survey. The couple had a baby girl, then headed west to Colorado. Their first daughter, Louise, grew up there, along with her two sisters. Louise is my mother-in-law.

"Jamma loved to go hiking," Sutay told me. "She carried a plant guide wherever she went," identifying plant species with her father's scientific curiosity and passion.

I was equally impressed by my wife's curiosity. It was genuine and she was following it, instead of letting these questions slip away. Her queries had led us to some amazing, memorable places so far, and here was one more. We emerged from Mussoorie's main stretch of shops and restaurants, and continued down a narrow, rain-dampened road, where we found the arched entrance to the Woodstock School and passed underneath.

The pine-shrouded campus was built on a steep hillside in the forest, its moss-stained buildings surrounded by a living canopy of trees and, in the moments when the clouds cleared, long views of the countryside. At the school office, Melanie, a British expat who'd been living abroad for twenty years and had two children attending the school, greeted us outside the teacher's lounge. Before we arrived, she had dug up Ellen's and Jean's school records and was delighted (not annoyed, as I'd feared) that we had come. "It validates my job as archivist," she said, handing us a folder labeled "Stewart—1938."

The folder was filled with school documents, letters, and photographs, some of which were singed black around the edges from a fire, adding a dramatic touch to the discovery. The documents had obviously been rescued in the nick of time, and now they were in our hands. We pored over Jamma's report cards, read notes from her father, took pictures, then followed Melanie on a tour of the campus, which felt modern and well kept. The place buzzed with 450 students—half Indian, we were told, the rest Nepalese, Tibetan, Bhutanese, American, and a handful of Koreans and Europeans.

We walked along the same pathways, under the same stone arches where Jamma had walked as a child, and we were glad we'd come.

————

That evening, however, we returned to the Bates Hotel to find the door to our room open a crack. Had we left it open…? We didn't think so, but the room seemed fine and we didn't realize anything was missing. The next morning, we found that one of our money belts was $500 lighter. The thieves had taken only the large bills and left the rest. Because we hadn't reported the open door the previous night, the man at the front desk said it was our fault that this had happened, saying over and over again, "It is impossible that someone entered your room. Impossible."

He stared at me as he said this, making eye contact even while doing the famous Indian head-bobble, half shake, half nod. He smiled, mocking my helpless glowering. Behind him, a trashy plastic religious icon sat on a shelf next to a candle and incense holder and played a prayer melody over and over again. The tune seared itself into my brain in those moments while I fumed.

"So who took our money, the monkeys?" I said.

The man smiled and bobbled his head as the chintzy little icon played its saintly tune.

THIRTEEN

City of joy

Our host organization in Calcutta had made reservations for us at the VIP Hotel in the northeastern outskirts of the city, near the airport on the desolate Kaikhali More. It had been chosen for its proximity to Jana Sanghati Kendra headquarters, which was still several public bus rides away.

It was a bizarre setting to begin the second phase of our honeymoon—volunteering for three months among tea workers in West Bengal. We settled into our room at the VIP just as the monsoon season got under way. It was damp and warm, but somehow homey. And it was temporary, one of many stepping-stones to get to our site assignment and begin our task.

We'd set the ball rolling months earlier, before we'd departed the U.S., when I asked Sutay one morning, "What about volunteering?"

What better way to approach a region as new and enormous and complex as India or Southeast Asia than by working with a host organization already established and trusted in the community? Volunteering would increase the chances for unplanned encounters and shared adversity—both surefire relationship strengtheners (or killers—we were aware of the risks).

Also, during our extended travels, volunteering would give us the excuse to take a break from constant movement, for short periods anyway, so we could experience a country as more than mere clients, customers, fares, and marks. It would give us a chance to learn customs and a few bits of languages, and to make friends with people we would never meet otherwise.

We had looked at our options for short-term volunteer opportunities, then submitted applications to American Jewish World Service (AJWS), a nonprofit international development organization based in New York City with ties to grassroots organizations around the world. In the AJWS Volunteer Corps, our professional skills—those of a nurse and a writer—would be matched with the specific project needs of a host organization. Somewhere.

They searched for a proper placement among the many organizations in their network and eventually decided to place us with Jana Sanghati Kendra—the People's Solidarity Center—a human rights organization based just north of Calcutta.

Calcutta, the one-time capital of the British Raj, officially Kolkata, or "Cal" by hipsters who live there, was at one time known as the "Paris of the East" for its trade in herbs, teas, and spices. Calcutta is an uber-city sprawled along the Hooghly River, which flows downstream into the tiger-inhabited

Sunderban swamps and the Bay of Bengal. It is a medley of styles, cultures, cuisines, languages, and politics, and it has produced India's greatest literary giants, classical poets, and revolutionaries. Chief among these is Rabindranath Tagore who wrote, "I slept and dreamt that life was joy. I awoke and saw that life was service. I acted and behold, service was joy."

I had also read that, in the last fifty years, so many rural families had inundated Calcutta, it had grown to be more famous for its decline into mass urbanism and slums than its short reign as a colonial jewel.

Yet, our hotel was removed from the wonders and problems of this great city. We were so close, yet so far. We looked out our room window at an empty urban landscape and swollen, gray clouds.

If we hadn't already, Sutay and I had now officially veered off any semblance of a tourist trail. No more backpacker hangouts, international Internet cafes, or banana pancakes for breakfast. And this was just the beginning, a week-long orientation in the relative luxuries of the VIP Hotel before heading to our work site farther north. We still had to travel fifteen hours by train to get to India's tea belt. We wouldn't have any fellow foreigners with whom to swap stories there, but we *would* have an apartment, a car and driver, translators, and a task to perform.

But first, Cal.

The Jana Sanghati Kendra office occupies a cramped, converted home in a residential area in the northern outskirts of

Calcutta. Anuradha Talwar, the director, greeted us at the door. She had a commanding presence, a strong voice, long black hair, and a flowing sari as she led us inside. The office had low ceilings, cluttered desks, ancient computers, file cabinets, and shoeless workers buzzing between rooms.

Anticipation buzzed between my wife and me as Anuradha picked up a piece of paper to read a description of our assignment. We sipped our tea and listened as the next chapter of our trip was revealed to us:

> Joshua and Sutay will be placed in a small town called Birpara to work in the plantations nearby. They will be studying the nutritional status of tea plantation workers who have just recovered from a long period of closure, leading to hunger and starvation deaths. Sutay could focus on the nutritional status of women and infants who have gone through this crisis. Joshua and Sutay will have a couple with them, Sarmishtha Biswas and Debasish Chokraborty, who have already done some work in the plantations. This couple will work with them as translators and local guides. They will also help with the study. It would be best if all four persons stayed in one house for security reasons. The volunteers will be required to travel to the plantations and back, generally by a hired car/motorcycles, as public transport is almost absent in the area.

"Are they here?" I asked, not even attempting to pronounce the names of Sarmishtha and Debasish, the two most important people in our new lives. Anuradha smiled and ushered us into the next room.

A short, jovial woman, dressed in a bright green *shalwar kameez* and yellow scarf draped low across her front, stood to greet us. Sutay wore a similar outfit, a burgundy and white *shalwar kameez* topped by dark shades and African-style *tiko* head wrap.

"I am Sarmishtha," she said. She and Debasish had just come back inside after smoking a cigarette on the patio. Sarmishtha was friendly and talkative, with a smoker's laugh and confident, liberated ease. Her hair was short and her eyes brown. Debasish was reserved and serious, a slim man with a beard and glasses. He shook hands firmly and silently.

"There should be no smoking in your house," said Anuradha.

"I agree," said Sutay, taking a stand, though we were both unsure of cultural norms around this.

"That will not be possible," Sarmishtha said, laughing at the silliness of such a thought.

These were our first impressions: Sarmishtha, a brash, stubborn, care-free, and independent woman; and Debasish, a mellow, scruffy, thoughtful man who didn't waste words. We'd get along just fine.

———

We spent the next five days commuting to the JSK office by bus and working nine to five in the office with our new colleagues, mostly composing the survey questionnaire we would use with the tea workers. We also got to know each other a little.

Debasish and Sarmishtha were both born and raised in Calcutta and had known each other since childhood. Debasish ran a small fishing cooperative in the south. It was one of several risky, labor-related ventures he was into. Sarmishtha lived with her extended family. She showed us photos of her new niece, and one morning she sang classic Bengali music to us with a stunning voice, then laughed when she realized people in the office were listening. She and Deba, as she called him, had a relaxed, brother-sisterly ease between them that made Sutay and me instantly comfortable—even though we still didn't want them to smoke cigarettes in the house.

In the evenings, my wife and I lounged in bed at the VIP, watching movies, listening to the rain outside, and breathing the mold. By the end of the first week, we'd had enough of this routine and decided to get out and finally see downtown Calcutta. Sarmishtha and Debasish had already departed for Birpara to secure an apartment and prepare for our arrival, so we were on our own in the big city.

We also thought it would be smart to squeeze in a date night before shacking up for the next three months in small quarters with our translators. You'd think our entire trip would feel like one long date, especially as newlyweds with no children, but like anything that continues for months on end, the length and routine of traveling eventually chipped away at some of its exotic romanticism. Routines become routines, even while traveling. So going out for the night in Calcutta was about more than just dinner. It was about keeping the sense of adventure and unpredictability of it all. Ten years down the road, settled in a deeper routine with children, this would be much more of a challenge. But on this night, all we had to do was launch ourselves into the city, then react to its stimuli—as a team.

To get downtown we boarded a city bus, which took us to the commercial mayhem of Sudder and Park Streets, giving us a long panorama view of Calcutta on its way through traffic. The sidewalks were crowded, the walls dotted with hammer-and-sickle graffiti.

We splurged on a "continental" meal of chicken and pasta at an overpriced, air-conditioned restaurant. We walked between bookshops and parks, tea stands and monuments. Mostly, we wondered at the sheer activity on the sidewalks. These were not merely spaces for people to walk. Calcutta sidewalks are also used to bathe, cut hair, clean teeth, run businesses, beg, and sleep. Near the subway entrance, a dark-skinned shirtless man crouched over a beehive he had brought from somewhere outside the city. A swarm of bees circled his head comfortably as customers handed him containers that he filled with honey and chunks of honeycomb.

After walking for a while, it was time for a drink. Birpara, where we were headed in a few days, was a dry province and we knew this could be our last chance for several months to sip an adult beverage. We stepped into a bar with a karaoke stage and a handful of customers, and bellied up. I had a beer and Sutay ordered rum and pineapple juice. Mine was cold and bitter and perfect. I was pondering its perfection when I saw Sutay's head lurch forward. Her fingers met her lips and came out with a wriggling cockroach that she threw onto the bar.

She'd forgotten to check her straw.

The bartender looked over with a noncommittal head waggle and a smile. Then my sweet, lovely wife did something I'll never forget. She put the straw down, lifted her glass, clinked it to my bottle, and drank her drink, the roach trying to pull itself from the sticky puddle of juice on the counter.

Perhaps some instinct should have made me disgusted with my mate's actions, which some would deem unsanitary. But I saw the exact opposite—Sutay's utterly practical behavior proved she would be a decisive and thrifty mother to my children, unwilling to waste a drop of precious resources (in this case, alcohol that had probably killed any germs from the roach anyway).

One drink was enough, and after a day of nonstop sounds, smells, and sights in Calcutta, we decided to call it a night. Rather than hire an expensive taxi to the VIP Hotel, we decided to try our luck on the Calcutta Metro Railway. We were standing on the sidewalk, searching for the subway entrance, when a short, bespectacled Good Samaritan on his way home from work stopped to help us.

"I am Pradeep," he said. "You will follow me."

He guided us through various tunnels and turnstiles, blocking for us as we pushed ourselves into the rush hour crowds and boarded the train. Pradeep got off after a few stops, leaving us with instructions to stay on till Dumdum, the last stop.

That's when we realized we had taken the wrong line entirely! Pradeep probably had no idea where the VIP Hotel was and had given us instructions just to save face. Who knew. Most of the train was empty by now and Sutay and I emerged, quite alone, from the Dumdum station into a drop-down monsoon downpour. We could barely hear each other as we shouted about what to do.

Picture my wife and me holding hands and running through ankle-deep rainwater outside the station, then leaning on each other, the water knee-deep now, dark and warm, sucking and pulling at our shoes. We jumped aboard a hand-pulled rickshaw whose driver pulled us out of the station area and deposited us in a taxi area. We got into a car, still lost, soaked, vulnerable, and being driven through Dumdum, a Calcutta neighborhood named for a bullet factory.

Sometimes the unknown of travel is romantic, mysterious, and subtle. Sometimes it crashes out of the sky and squishes between your toes, reminding you that you are far, far from home—and that anyone who squishes along by your side is someone you should keep close for a long time.

FOURTEEN

Tea is meant to be bitter

The smell of fresh, fermenting chlorophyll was thick in the air as we followed the manager past the leaf-sorting machines. Churning industrial-age gears and presses made an enormous ruckus, and trucks drove around, dumping and loading tea leaves at all the various stages of production, from seed to final product.

Suddenly, the plantation manager stopped in his tracks and stared at the "Honey Vanilla Chamomile" label dangling from the rim of Sutay's plastic travel mug. *"That* is not tea!" he said to her. She had brought a stash of Colorado-based Celestial Seasonings in a zip-lock in her backpack. We hadn't expected any trouble.

Pakistan and India are the world's top producers *and* con-
sumers of tea, both creating and feeding a global thirst for it.
During our trip, charcoal-heated pots of tea appeared constantly and out of nowhere. Once, in the narrow lanes of the
Birpara market, my laundry *wallah* bought me a 5-rupee shot
of *chai* to drink while he folded my clothes.

Most Indians we met drank powdered black tea, spiced with
cloves and drowned in ultra-sweetened, hot milk. Tea sellers
ladled it from cream-crusted cauldrons into throwaway ceramic cups that you smashed on the train tracks when you
were finished. These were being replaced with white plastic
cups, which carpeted the ground around each station.

Each of the thousand cups of tea we drank was as different
as the person who served it and the vessel in which it came. But
they all had one thing in common, as the garden manager was
so insistent on reminding us: Real tea contains the crushed,
dried, and fermented leaves of the *Camellia sinensis* tree. That
was tea.

Not herbs.

Tea.

I am a coffee drinker, and I spent most of our trip patiently
surviving in tea country. I hadn't realized such vast swaths of
coffee-free territories existed. From Pakistan across the entire
Indian subcontinent, a stale sprinkling of Nescafé was the closest thing to coffee available for thousands of miles. Except for
a short java-friendly detour in Southeast Asia (thank God for

Laos!), I had to make do for many, many coffee-free months. But that was fine. I was, for the time being, a tea drinker and might as well learn all I could about the stuff.

"Come!" commanded the manager, waving us to follow him out of the office. Sarmishtha, Debasish, Sutay, and I followed. He was a clean-cut, slim man, who wore white shorts and high white socks up to his knees, the old British colonial outfit.

Decades before, British writer V.S. Naipaul had written: "The tea gardens are now Indian-owned, but little has changed. Indian caste attitudes perfectly fit plantation life and clannishness of the planters' clubs…The tea workers remain illiterate, alcoholic, lost, a medley of tribal people without traditions and now…even without a language, still strangers in the land, living not in established villages but…in shacks strung along estate roads."

In some parts of the Indian tea growing world, we observed, his description was still true, both of the clannish Indian manager whose ridiculous knobby knees stuck out of his socks and of conditions on the "labor lines" and strung-out shacks where the workers lived. This was Dooars, the region where, 150 years ago, the British first planted tea and where my wife and I now found ourselves, at the beginning of a three-month project conducting a health survey of a sample of workers.

But first we needed permission from each of the six plantations we'd selected, which is why we were walking politely behind the self-important manager on a tour of his facilities.

———

The activity and sheer volume of leaves here was impressive, especially after visiting a closed garden that morning, one of the plantations that had shut down. That had been a place of quiet, hot despair, where thousands of workers and their families were without income, health services, and reliable food and water.

At this garden, things were active, buzzing, alive. Still, as we continued our tour, Knobby Knees kept berating my wife. "Chamomile is not tea!" he yelled above the machines. "Mint is not tea! Only *tea* is tea! And it is *not* served in bags! Have you ever looked at what is inside a bag?!" he asked, not waiting for an answer. "Tear open a 'tea' bag and look at what you are drinking!"

He walked us to the roasting rooms with their toasty odors and clouds of fine tea dust that made us sneeze. Sutay continued nodding politely, maintaining a placid smile for the man, but then I saw her begin to bristle and I hoped he didn't push it.

"What's the best way to prepare a pot of tea?" I asked, trying to distract him with his own vast knowledge.

"The perfect cup?" he began. "First, you place two-point-five grams of tea for every fifty milliliters of water!"

He was pleased I was taking notes and nodded his approval as he went on. "This you are heating to one hundred degrees Celsius, then steeping for five minutes, covered, in a neutral ceramic or porcelain pot! Tea is very sensitive! It is picking up the flavor of anything you are putting it in, even the flavor of a cigarette smoked in the same room! For that reason we are not allowing cigarettes inside our factory!" He looked around, daring Sarmishtha and Debasish to light up.

"What about sugar and cream?" I asked.

He pointed to a quote on the wall by George Orwell. "How can you call yourself a true tea lover if you destroy the flavour of your tea by putting sugar in it? It would be equally reasonable to put in pepper or salt. Tea is meant to be bitter, just as beer is meant to be bitter. If you sweeten it, you are no longer tasting the tea, you are merely tasting the sugar; you could make a very similar drink by dissolving sugar in plain hot water."

I watched Sarmishtha and Debasish nod in agreement, and I sensed that our days of drinking sweetened *doodh chai* milk tea had come to an end. A worker arrived with a tray of cups, filled with dark, hot, bitter-fresh tea.

In Dooars, our home for the next three months, tea was everything. It was time, money, and food; tea was a drink, a business, a culture, a place. And all was not well in the tea world.

The Indian tea industry was in crisis, and had been for a few years. Global prices were down and local plantations were going out of business left and right. There was competition from China and Africa. Maoist rebels from Nepal were said to be infiltrating the labor lines, and reports of starvation deaths weren't good for anybody. I understood Knobby Knees' testiness. Here we were, a group of foreigners and labor activists from Calcutta, poking around, talking to the workers, taking pictures, carrying clipboards. He was right to be wary.

The history of tea in India is a familiar story to that of many cash crops around the world. First, colonizers decimated forests to plant expanses of said cash crop for export. Then they rounded up communities of indigenous people to plant and pick it, resettling them on plantations where managers had complete control over wages and conditions—and where they could literally breed an endless succession of future leaf plucker generations. In 1947, the terms of India's independence transferred management of all businesses, including tea companies, from the British to the Indians, many of whom were shortsighted businessmen from other parts of the country and who caused more than twenty businesses, or gardens, in Dooars to close their doors by 2003.

When we arrived in 2005, descendants of the original Atavasi and Nepali labor forces were *still* doing the planting and plucking—or they weren't, with no work and no income, isolated in company-owned villages where the health care, schools, electricity, and water had all been shut off when the plants closed. The only other work available was crushing rocks by hand at quarries across the river in Bhutan.

***

We left the manager's office and continued our tour of the plantation outside. We breathed the fresh air of the tea fields and watched a nearby group of pickers, only their shoulders and heads visible above the flat table of plants. Their faces were drawn. Several women had infants slung across their backs as they plucked and stashed, plucked and stashed. Though the sky was bright blue, most of the women carried closed umbrellas balanced horizontally atop head loads, in case of downpours.

The woman nearest us had on a bright red dress and head cloth, her arms brown and blurred as they swept across the plants, removing only the yellow shoots, the part of the plant that would ferment correctly. Where the pluckers had already worked, the tea leaves left behind were dark, shiny green; in front of them, the color was lighter. The worker with the red dress threw fistfuls of tea into a sack hanging from her forehead on a plastic tumpline. When her bag was full, she carried it to the end of her row, to a foreman and a waiting truck.

———

Back in his office, the manager agreed to allow us to include his garden in our survey, as a control, since his business was still operating and we would be able to compare it favorably to the closed gardens. But he also told us that our mission to document hunger in the region was "useless."

"I can tell you what you will find," he said. "These people are not civilized. They are not like you and me."

I watched Sarmishtha bite her tongue. Later, as we drove through the fields, she exploded. "What we will find is disgusting and unstaffed hospitals! We will find wages and rations in arrears. We will find no child-care facilities and no breaks for breastfeeding women. That is what we will find!"

FIFTEEN

Of surveys and samosas

During the first few weeks, we settled in, got oriented, and established trust with our local contacts—as much as we could in that short a time, anyway. Our task was to interview 120 families of tea workers and to write a report on what we found. We requested and gained permission to survey families in six different gardens and drew up a rough timeline for our work. We would interview twenty families in each garden.

On paper, it was a perfect short-term volunteer project. The health survey would utilize both Sutay's clinical knowledge and public health experience and my writing and document-editing skills. In addition, the project had a training and interchange component between us and our local counterparts,

Sarmishtha and Debasish, who, as a result of the survey, would strengthen relationships with worker groups in the area, gather important data, and attract international attention to the crisis in Dooars.

For the first few surveys, the four of us worked together as we interviewed the families, developing our protocol and ironing out kinks in the questions. After a few days of this, we split into pairs to cover twice the ground, Sarmishtha and I taking one row, Sutay and Debasish another.

Our rounds on the labor lines of active tea gardens began around four in the afternoon, when the workers came home from the fields, processing plants, and packaging factories. At some gardens, before visiting the workers in their homes to ask our questions and take our measurements, we paid a visit to the local union boss, whose blessing we required, and who often served us tea and cookies while his family looked on.

After the formalities, we walked from house to house, asking families about their health, the conditions on their garden, what they'd eaten in the last 24 hours, and what (if any) relief services they were receiving.

How many people are in your family?

What is your job? (Plucker, Spray Worker, Factory Worker, Truck Driver, Water Fetcher, Gardener/ Pruner)

Has your family gone a full day without eating in the last year?

What is your drinking water source? (Tube Well, Well, River, Rain Water, Supply Water, Pond)

Is anybody in your family currently pregnant or breastfeeding?

Does the garden provide a *creche* [nursery]?

How many family members are currently suffering from diarrhea or vomiting?

How many family members have died in the last three years?

After repeating the questions, taking family portraits, calculating calories, and accepting more cups of tea, the four of us would meet back at the vehicle. Sometimes our work ran into the night and we'd have to find our way to the van with my headlamp, swatting at the cloud of monstrous insects it drew.

In the back of the van, Sutay, Sarmishtha, Debasish, and I faced each other, shelling peanuts and bouncing like popcorn as Mani dodged potholes, trucks, and cows while negotiating gravelly riverbeds and confusing road grids to get us back to Birpara. We used this time to collate our data sheets and organize the equipment while I ticked off how many families we'd covered and how many we had to go.

When it was dark on the narrow garden roads, Mani grew nervous about *haati*, wild elephants, which had been seen in this area. Debasish teased him about it. "Maniiii," Debasish would sing cruelly, "there are *haati* ahead!" The poor guy would choke on the *paan* he was chewing as he looked around in fright.

On closed gardens, we learned, it didn't matter what time we started because nobody there was working. We headed out as early as we could on those days, to do our rounds and return to Birpara before the heat of the day. We would pick up a to-go bag of samosas at Lovely's Sweets, then bump across the train tracks and into the long, green tea fields.

SIXTEEN

Bulbulda will arrange

Birpara, West Bengal, was a nondescript tea-growing town near the Bhutan border. It was tiny by Indian standards, about 40,000 people living in a smallish grid of neighborhoods built around the intersection of two highways and a rail line. There were neither restaurants nor attractions, but there were a few scattered temples and shrines, each located near a flag-strewn bodhi tree surrounded by boxlike dwellings and auto repair shops. Around the town, extending in every direction, were flat-pruned fields of tea, an endless ocean of green.

Sutay and I moved into a two-story apartment building called Akhil Bhavan. We had our own room, a bed with a mosquito net, and a barred window that looked out over an overgrown lot and the post office, where we would have packages sewn up in fabric and sealed with wax to send treasures home to our futures selves.

There, in Akhil Bhavan, we joined an eclectic, warm cast of characters. We joked about writing a sitcom called the *The Bengali Bunch,* featuring our new friends and our zany adventures.

First and foremost, Sarmishtha and Debasish: our roommates, translators, cooks, guides, teachers, and friends. The two of them and the two of us were strangers in a strange land together; they were from the big city, Calcutta, 500 miles to the south. The four of us would spend thousands of hours together, laughing and talking and eating in our shared apartment: a two-bedroom, half-kitchen, one bathroom (bucket bath and squat toilet). Not to mention the time together in the back of our white van, our "tea-mobile," which carried us on ridiculous routes across the district.

Within weeks, the four of us had our own inside jokes, including Sarmishtha's euphemism, "Some pressure is there," which she said politely in the van, blushing as the smell filled the small space and we dove to open the windows. The phrase instantly became our go-to fart joke.

Bodi, which actually means "sister-in-law," lived with her family in the apartment next door. She was a large, protective, mother-hen figure, in charge of filtering our drinking water and paying our sweeper girl. Bodi breastfed her thin-legged adopted 4-year-old, Shanko, named after the conch shell used by Hin? to call their deities. She had a loud voice and an ?sity that kept her popping into our apartment ` the day and night, to Sutay's frustration. Her ("big brother"), was a smiling, white-teethed, big-haired insurance salesman who sold policies for houses, cars, and cows.

But the most important character of them all was Vikash Roy, a.k.a. Bulbul, "the nightingale" in Bengali. We followed Sarmishtha and Debasish's lead and added the affectionate "da" to his name, short for "elder brother." Bulbulda was our uncle, our fixer, and the owner of the white minivan. Bulbulda hired our driver, Mani, who loved to chew *paan*, a mixture of betel nut and bitter spices wrapped in a leaf. Mani chewed and spat while squatting by the tire every time we stopped to take pictures or pick up supplies. After three weeks, Mani was fired for taking private taxi fares on our gasoline dollar.

Bulbulda was all-powerful, using his network of connections in Birpara to accomplish anything we needed. He used to work in the tea industry, so he helped with our list of gardens and manager contacts. I fully realized Bulbulda's godfather status when Debasish and Sarmishtha repeatedly responded to so many of my questions with, "Bulbulda will arrange."

I needed a custom writing desk to work on my laptop. "Don't worry, Bulbulda will arrange." Next thing I knew, I was in a carpenter's workshop near the market, sitting in a chair and testing imaginary table heights as Bulbul and my entourage stood around. He nodded approvingly as the carpenters noted the measurements and he negotiated a fair price with them on my behalf.

Sutay remarked that some plants would be nice in our house. Sarmishtha said, "Bulbulda will arrange." Potted flowers appeared within hours.

We settled into a rhythm in Akhil Bhavan. For breakfast we ate toast and sipped dark, unsweetened, tall glasses of tea; for lunch, we sat cross-legged on cane mats and ate Deba's egg curry and rice; for dinner, another round of egg curry and rice, maybe with a slightly different vegetable combination.

Many days, especially during those first few weeks, Bulbulda would stroll unannounced into our flat and plop down on the cement floor to smoke a cigarette, drink tea, and help plan the logistics of the following day's "program."

"Tomorrow," Bulbul would announce, "the program will begin at 9. Tomorrow, you will go to Katalbari, a closed garden."

Sometimes he ate; the five of us would sit in a circle on the floor picking up clumps of rice and egg curry with the fingers of our right hands. The first day he said, "You cannot truly taste the food unless you eat it with your fingers."

Sometimes he came in the evening after sending Mani out for quasi-legal alcohol and cigarettes. On those nights, we drank warm beer while Deba and Sarmishtha chain-smoked, and, if we were lucky, performed for us. Sarmishtha sang classical hypnotic Bengali melodies while Deba played tabla beats on a plastic bucket.

When the power went out in the building, which happened a handful of times, the four of us walked five blocks to Lovely's Sweets, the closest thing Birpara had to an eatery. The owner, Sanjay, had a generator, so he stayed open during outages, and we would order short cups of milky *ca*, Bengali for tea, pronounced "cha" and tin plates of deep-fried *gulab jamun* dumplings soaked in honey. Lovely's was more like a sweet shop and fast-food *dhaba* whose breakfast specialty was *puri*, or runny, spiced lentils poured over greasy rounds of fried dough. In the morning, we had to brave the transport area in front of the market, which meant dodging bicycle rickshaws, jeeps, and pedestrians to get to the counter at Lovely's. But in the evening, it was less of a mad rush. Lovely's was also reliable for a plate of *momos*, Nepali-style stuffed noodles, which we craved, served with a red chili sauce.

I loved dipping our toes into this life, Sutay and I, merging together with new people in new places so easily. It was intense and hot and easy and slow, this life, and we witnessed some really horrible and beautiful things; people starving and sick, people smiling and warm.

I especially enjoyed the few times when I got to watch Sutay work in our labor-line. Sometimes Sarmishtha and I finished our assigned families before Sutay and Deba, and we would join them; on these occasions, I watched my wife from afar, watched her put people at ease while weighing or measuring or asking her questions. Her bedside manner was filled with compassion, and I watched her subjects react to it by softening and smiling.

I am a lucky man, I thought to myself (for the hundredth time since we began our trip). It was a wonderful, easy mantra to keep as I watched her close her clipboard and look across the patio to me. Yet another amazing aspect of my partner had revealed itself before my eyes, and I was even more in love. Even when she approached us and broke the spell by whispering to Sarmishtha, "Some pressure is there," which I'm sure was released amid our sudden burst of loud laughter, drawing even more stares than normal from the villagers.

SEVENTEEN

Durga Puja

Each day, as Sutay and I walked up Mahatma Gandhi Road, the main drag in Birpara which led from our apartment to the bus stand and Lovely's Sweets, we watched as human, animal, and god figures appeared inside makeshift statue workshops along the length of the street. Most of the workshops were in open-door garages. The people were preparing for Durga Puja, the largest celebration of the year in northeast India. It is a rowdy ten-day festival with layers of ceremony, ritual, and activities, which coincide with the end of the monsoon—and this time with the end of our three-month volunteer assignment in Birpara.

The sculpted gods along M.G. Road began as rough straw-and-wire figures, then progressed into sculpted mud and their features began to take shape—muscle-bound arms and legs, elephant snouts and ears, fierce tiger faces. Finally, bright paint, wigs, clothes, and other props were used to complete the menagerie. Sometimes the figures were placed in the street to dry in the sun, and we grew accustomed to walking among deranged demons and animals on our way to buy a plate of *momos* or catch a bus. Durga has ten arms and is usually depicted with an entourage of beasts and fellow gods, including Ganesha, the elephant-headed deity, and Saraswati with her peacock. For three months, Sutay and I watched as local artists created different versions of this cast of festival icons.

As we neared the end of our time in Birpara, the figures neared completion. Sarmishtha and Debasish departed for Calcutta to celebrate Durga Puja with their families, and Bulbulda, our local guide and godfather, had promised to take care of us in Birpara. He had already helped me shop for a proper outfit to wear during the festivities (a royal purple *kameez* and white baggy pants), and he had the entire week-long festival planned out for us.

Durga is a Hindu goddess, the primary consort of Shiva the Destroyer, source of the universe. Dominique Lapierre wrote in *City of Joy* that Durga's father, "Himalaya, King of the mountains, provided her with a lion as a mount, then the moon gave her a rounded face and death her long black hair. She was the color of dawn."

Neighborhood clubs commissioned each set of Durga statues. They raised money by going door to door with a bucket, after which each club threw a series of enormous parties. Central to these parties was displaying a proper pantheon on a bamboo-framed structure called a *pandal*, constructed specifically for Durga Puja. Sutay and I donated to the first few clubs that came asking, then realized we had to stop or we'd go broke.

On the first day of Durga Puja, the gods, lions, and devils were transported across town in the backs of flatbed trucks amid much drumming and dancing. That's how the whole event began, with each set of statues slowly parading down the street and then arriving on its *pandal*. All of Birpara lined up to watch as the deities passed. That evening, the figures in place, it was time to go out and visit the *pandals*.

We began our rounds at Durgabari, in the lanes behind our apartment. There were firecrackers, food carts, and loud music. A vibrant, safe sense of community pervaded, the relaxed feeling of an entire village blowing off steam. Inside the Durgabari tent, we found suffused yellow sunlight and a crowd gathering around the sparkling god figures. Durga rode a roaring lion in full gallop as she stabbed a mustachioed demon, lanced a cobra, and stepped on a buffalo, all with a beatific, motherly look on her face. Small piles of shoes sat below the raised platform, and men and women kneeled and chanted amid incense and butter candles. Some left money on the floor and received a blessing from the priest sitting on the edge of the stage.

Outside, a happy air of homecoming pervaded the picnicky scene. Family members had returned home for Durga Puja from school or from jobs at call centers in Calcutta. Young soldiers on leave from the front in Kashmir had also come home for the celebration. Sutay and I were invited to join in, and we did, with a little pang of sadness for the year's worth of our own family gatherings, holidays, and births that we were missing during our journey.

Even though we'd been in Birpara for three months, many people—especially Birparians who had just returned from abroad—were surprised to find two Americans in their midst. Our oddity and local fame flared up during our exploration of the festival. People stared; they asked to take photos with us and we obliged. They were curious, eager, friendly, sometimes even protective, offering to escort us to the next *pandal* or to retrieve us from our home for the following day's events.

In the Durgabari food tent, volunteers served us small plates of *kichuri*—or "hodge-podge"—a ubiquitous dish of rice, lentils, and chilies. For most of the year in Birpara, *kichuri* is like what mac 'n cheese is in the West, a simple, gut-full of comfort carbs. Our housemate, Debasish, made it often, usually with a side of curried mixed vegetables, the gravy of which is essential when the *kichuri* is sticky or dry. During *puja* time, however, *kichuri* is elevated to a ritualistic dish, whose preparation is a major part of the competition between neighborhood clubs. In each tent, *kichuri* was served from aluminum buckets onto tiny plates made from brown sewn-together leaves. These "plates" were sprinkled with water when diners returned them and were reused.

That first day we accepted all invitations, eating plate after plate of *kichuri* and eventually landing in the inner chamber of the Kali Temple among a circle of young men. We all scooped handfuls of lumpy *kichuri* into tight, extended bellies. After eating, Ajay Guha, president of the biggest *pandal* club in Birpara and owner of Lovely's Sweets, offered to send a meal of his famous *kichuri* to our home the next day.

"To nourish you," he said, for the coming days of *pandal* walking. We thanked him and went home to rest.

True to Ajay's word, the next day, eight teenage boys showed up at our door, smiling and waving through the window. They greeted us one by one, shaking our hands and trying out their English. I took the warm package of food from them and promised to visit their *pandal*.

On this night, Bulbulda, had promised to bring his wife, Bodi, to accompany our rounds. When they arrived, we invited them in. Bodi wore a red, orange, and black sari, and Bulbul wore a yellow-collared shirt and blue jeans. Sutay came out of the bedroom, absolutely gorgeous in a thigh-length white *kameez* over her nylon, quick-dry expedition pants; she had a violet scarf positioned just so over her chest, her long hair in a single braid. Bodi placed a sparkling *bindi* between Sutay's eyes and her outfit was complete.

Our neighbors entered, also dressed to the nines, and I taught everyone the custom of dipping apples in honey to usher in a sweet New Year, since, in addition to Durga Puja, it was Rosh Hashanah, the Jewish New Year, that night. I told them that where I was from, it was also a holiday called "Rosh Hashanah Puja." Bulbulda responded with a warm New Year's embrace and kind wishes for my family at home.

"Dhonnobaad," I said, using one of the few Bengali words I'd learned. Thank you.

We walked far and wide that night, visiting at least ten *pandals* with Bulbul as our guide. At one point, he took us to a curious shrine in front of an old tree. It was a fertility shrine, he said. The stone mound, he said, represented Shiva's lingam, the godly phallus, as it entered a divine yoni. Then Bulbul snickered something in Bengali to Bodi, pointing in our direction. Sutay blushed on cue.

After several hours, Sutay and Bodi both needed a restroom. Bulbulda led us to a latrine behind the elementary school. I could smell it from twenty feet away. It was a doozy of an outhouse, leaning like the Pisser of Pisa in a clump of tall, forbidding weeds.

Now, misadventures with the toilets of the world typically come in two forms: (1) encounters with dreadful public toilets like this one, and (2) bathroom stories from the bush, in which a traveler's desire to avoid said nasty public toilets results in memorable experiences.

On this evening, Sutay refused to enter the outhouse that Bulbulda had chosen, even though Bodi had used it without a problem. Instead, my wife opted for an open-air *hishi* behind the latrine, which I told her was a bad idea. Bulbul and I exchanged glances as she ignored us, high-stepping into the dark grass, which she'd decided was preferable to the unlit horrors in the tiny shack. All went well until she was returning and suddenly disappeared before my eyes.

Bulbulda and I ran, skidding to a stop at the edge of a ditch. We pulled Sutay out of thigh-deep, black drainage flowing from the outhouse. I expected tears, shrieks, and demands to be taken home. I held my breath—partly in anticipation of what would happen and partly because my beloved smelled like diarrhea.

"Bulbulda," she said. "Please take me to the nearest water source."

No one spoke as we walked. There were chunks hanging off Sutay's pants; the tails of her beautiful white shirt were ruined. The worst part was hearing her toes squish in her shoes; I thought I saw the hint of a tear in the corner of her eye, but it never fell.

A good traveler rolls with the punches and keeps smiling. I had seen this in Sutay over and over again on this trip—when she fell sick in Islamabad, when she found glass in her rice (by biting into it) in New Delhi, or, my favorite, when she sucked a live cockroach through a straw at a bar in Calcutta. My point? Sutay had proven her mettle many times over, so I already knew she was tough, but on that final night of Durga Puja, in a small West Bengali border town, she earned her India traveler's stripes once and for all.

Bulbulda stopped to purchase a bar of soap at a corner shop and handed it to me. I gave it to Sutay when we arrived at the train station, where Bulbulda had said there was a public water pump. We could hear the music and festival noises from the train platform as I worked the hand pump and Sutay scrubbed her pants, legs, and feet. When she was finished, she posed for a photo in front of a public service announcement that read, in English, "CLEANLINESS IS NEXT TO GODLINESS!" Only then did Bulbul, Bodi, and I allow ourselves to break into laughter, and Sutay joined in.

———

The next morning, I awoke to someone yelling into the window, "Shubho Bijoya!"

This was the standard greeting between everybody on the final, most important day of Durga Puja: Bijoya. "Shubho

Bijoya!" is used among friends and with strangers, accompa-
nied by a special only-for-Bijoya hug—a three-part embrace.
Bulbulda was outside, and while Sutay stayed in bed, I got up
and walked with him to Lovely's Sweets.

"Shubho Bijoya!" I said to Ajay, who smiled and brought us
tea. We watched as crews loaded the Durga idols onto trucks
again.

Bijoya, explained Bulbulda, was the grand finale. Throughout West Bengal, thousands of Durga idols were paraded back
through town in another riot of drumming, dust, and dance
before being taken to the nearest river and cast into the current. (Weeks later we would see the gruesome-looking remains
of these statues far downstream in Calcutta, soaked mud-and-
straw goddess figures clinging like corpses to the banks of the
Hooghly River.)

"Sent back to her husband's house," Bulbul said. "Maa
Durga comes from the house of her parents and she returns to
the house of her husband, Shiva," he continued. "*Bijoya* means
'victory.' This *puja* is about the destruction of evil."

But on this afternoon, Bulbulda and I watched as drum
troupes paraded by and we drank our tea. He leaned back in
his chair, squinted, and pulled hard on a cigarette. Hindu rites
sometime seem complicated because of the noise and confu-
sion and multifaceted multitude of gods. But sometimes they
are simple. Durga kills her demon. So can each of us.

"The next *puja* is this Sunday," said Bulbulda. "It is Lakshmi
Puja, the god of wealth and prosperity. The day you leave."

"Is it like Durga Puja?" I asked.

"No. It is a quiet *puja*. With family, in homes."

That Sunday, our last day in Birpara, Sutay and I walked Mahatma Gandhi Road one last time. The workshops were quiet and empty, but a crowd had gathered next to a small shrine to Sunni, or Saturn. A long-haired, shirtless priest was speaking to a small gathering, and we stopped to watch. He mixed water, flower petals, and spices in a cup made of folded leaves and, with his fingers, flung droplets into the crowd. We lowered our heads as we saw everyone else do, and received the cool drops on our necks.

"Om shanti, shanti, shanti," said the priest. "Peace, peace, peace."

We walked on to the station, where we placed our bags in a pile and waited for the train.

EIGHTEEN

One last cup

We had had some good times with Bulbulda and our crew in Birpara, but despite so many friendships, smiles, and silver buckets of *kichuri*, our time in tea country will always be most defined by malarial faces, sick babies, and stories of death. One of our jobs, in fact, as we walked the labor lines and inspected garden hospitals, was to collect "verbal autopsies" to ensure that the details went on the record. Sometimes the stories we heard were detailed; sometimes the families did not have much to say.

Even after hundreds of reports of starvation deaths, they are difficult to document. This is because people rarely perish directly from starvation—they die of other things, like diarrhea and malaria, which easily ravage a body weakened by hunger. Here is an example from our report:

Sunita M. was 3 years old when she died in 2003, soon after closure of the garden where her parents worked. She was stricken with "disease," said her mother, Gita, who works today on the reopened garden. "Then her body swelled, then she died."

The family struggled after that, sometimes collecting ferns and other plants from the nearby jungle for food. Less than one year after Sunita's death, Gita's youngest son, Akosh, seven months old, came down with diarrhea that would not go away. She fed him both breast milk and cow milk, but he continued to suffer. There was "nobody in the garden hospital," she said, and they had no money to travel to Birpara or buy medicine. Two months after he first became sick, Akosh also died.

Akosh and Sunita were among six reported deaths under four years of age on this garden. Sibram M. was 1 year old when he died of diarrhea soon after closure, suffering for one month because there was no medicine in the garden hospital, no mobile medical van, and no money to go anywhere else. Anisa M. died of vomiting and diarrhea at the age of 2; she was taken to Birpara Hospital, but by then it was too late. The compounder could do nothing for Baby N., who became "sick and wouldn't stop crying" and died 15 days after his birth. Baby M. developed a "blood cough at one month, and passed away the next day."

Things were especially bad on the plantations that had closed for business. There we found zero to little relief services being provided, just as Sarmishtha had predicted we would. On some functioning gardens, the government provided meals for the children, but these lunch programs were not always reliable.

And what did we do about it? We rode around the tea gardens, measuring people's weight and height, taking notes about their diet, and documenting death. I was sometimes frustrated that our job was *not* to provide relief, only record data. I watched my wife kneel beside children, smiling at them while noting signs of malnutrition.

Whether she is helping a woman through labor in a modern hospital in Baltimore, Maryland, or weighing a scared 2-year-old in a mud-floor hut in India, Sutay is particularly good at calming and reassuring people. If only she had been able to do more. Instead, she jotted down a few numbers, then asked the next child to step on the scale.

Development work is a balancing act between short-term Band-Aids and long-term solutions. In the end, I'm glad we were working toward the latter. Our final report, "Nutritional Survey of Tea Workers on Closed, Re-opened, and Open Tea Plantations of The Dooars Region, West Bengal, India," concluded:

> Malnutrition exists on all six gardens surveyed. Even workers on open gardens endure lean periods due to decreased or delayed wage payments and food rations, as well as inconsistently provided benefits that they are due by law. Based on World Health Organization criteria for Body Mass Index, all four open gardens surveyed can be labeled as "starving communities" or "at critical risk for mortality from starvation."

Our host organization, Jana Sanghati Kendra, would send this document to the International Union of Food Workers in Geneva, Switzerland, resulting in funding for Sarmishtha and Debasish to continue their work with the people of Birpara. This was crucial. Not only did it mean our work would remain important after we left, but we wanted the best for our friends. Sarmishtha and Debasish were passionate about helping people and skilled at what they did. They deserved to be able to continue the work. We'd seen how they commanded a crowd whenever they showed up at a garden. People trusted them and sought them out for answers. Some days, groups of tea workers would show up at our Birpara apartment with questions about relief programs and how to apply for benefits. Sutay and I would emerge from our bedroom to find our home flooded with wide-eyed workers sitting on our living room floor while Sarmishtha and Debasish gave advice.

"Our goal is not just to help them get relief. It is to get these gardens reopened," said Debasish one day. "But first, the workers must have a little food in their bellies, and they must overcome the grief for dead family members. After that, they want nothing more than to work, to earn a living."

"The workers do not want to be beggars," Sarmishtha added. "That is not the way."

NINETEEN

Darjeeling

As we rolled through the tea fields toward Siliguri, I wondered, *Why is there so much suffering among tea growers in Dooars?* The only other situation I'd seen which remotely compares to the tea industry in Dooars is the coffee industry in Nicaragua. There, coffee production also has a long, exploitative history consisting of colonial hierarchies, profit-skimming middlemen, and disempowered, malnutritioned workers on whose backs the entire industry depended.

But I'd also watched as groups of Nicaraguan coffee growers benefited from a mini-revolution, targeting high-paying niche markets with high-quality, organic, fair trade, and bird-friendly certifications. They'd formed successful cooperatives and used newfound profits to build bridges, schools, and clinics in their communities. Could something like this be happening in India?

If there was anywhere we could answer this question, it was in Darjeeling, the fabled Himalayan outpost on the Silk Road to China, and whose very name is synonymous with quality tea. Because of its higher-altitude climate and unique soil makeup, Darjeeling is an epicenter for rare tea and alternative farming techniques. There were 69 registered tea gardens in Darjeeling District the year we visited, plus hordes of tea buyers, tea auctioneers, tea shop *wallahs*, international tea certifiers, and nongovernmental organizations working on sustainable tea production.

Darjeeling is another hill station with a large Nepali population and crowds of tourists from the lowlands. In Siliguri, we found a jeep headed to Darjeeling and climbed into the back with an extended family from Calcutta who carried wool blankets against the chill and drizzle of November. At the top of the mountain was a steep, cluttered town straddling a narrow ridge. Nepal and Mount Everest were somewhere to the west, Sikkim territory and Mount Kanchenjunga dominated to the northern horizon, and Bhutan lay to the east. Even though most of the high peaks were obscured in clouds during our time there, after the hot plains of Birpara, the moisture felt magical.

We found a cheap, clean guest house and set out to explore. It was so cold, the first thing we did was buy yak wool sweaters and hats. Then we walked through drizzle and fog to the summit of the highest point in town. There, beneath thousands of prayer flags in the town park, local teenagers smoked joints and told us about their crappy call center jobs in Calcutta.

When the rain fell harder, Sutay and I ducked into the Windamere Hotel, a stuffy, creaky-wood, colonial relic that had been built two centuries before as "a cozy boarding house for bachelor English and Scottish tea planters," then converted into a hotel before World War II. We walked into a cozy, heated parlor and sat down amid antique furniture, paintings, and carpets in front of a coal fire. The change from outside was so severe that it felt like we'd walked onto a movie set, and we hammed it up, lifting our noses and pinkies as we sniffed around and read the framed sign next to the fireplace out loud: "Visitors are requested not to take off their footwear, or put their feet on the furniture, or lie supine on the hearth, or sleep behind the settees, lest unintended offence be given to others."

A white-gloved server appeared and waggled his head. "We'll have the tea," I said.

The pots came covered in thick oven-mitt cozies with a card advising, "We recommend that you do not dilute this tea with milk. You may sweeten it, although many connoisseurs of tea would prefer that you drink it 'straight.' Before sipping, inhale the distinctive perfume of your tea to heighten your enjoyment of one of the world's great beverages."

We reclined in our chairs and sipped perfect, earthy, leafy-fresh Darjeeling tea from the fields outside in the rain. Cucumber sandwiches, scones, and pastries adorned the tray before us. I wolfed them down while Sutay daintily nibbled, and we drank cup after cup of tea.

———

During the next few days, I interviewed several garden managers and tea industry gurus, but felt no closer to even suggesting a solution for the starving pluckers down in Dooars. Part of it came down to that old development crux again: i.e, short-term relief vs. long-term sustainability. That is, how can we expect to implement deep-rooted solutions when people are sick and barely surviving?

One day Sutay and I hiked several miles downhill to tour a nearby cooperative and participate in their nascent homestay program. We trekked skinny trails from garden to garden, walking past tea operations, which were unrecognizable from the plantations we'd seen in Dooars. Instead of long, flat-topped, mono-cropped fields of tea, these were robust tea bushes on cool, green slopes, planted alongside a variety of other crops. Funds from a fair trade certification program had been used after the last harvest to build a bridge across one steep ravine, and they were working on funding a schoolhouse next.

At night Sutay and I ate with our host family in their kitchen. We squatted on the floor and learned a few Nepali phrases. I drank homemade beer, which was warm and gritty. Inviting tourists to stay in guest rooms was another way that growers could diversify their income, providing other sources of revenue when global tea prices slumped.

The home was warm, so different from the homes on the labor lines of Dooars, where desperation had clung to everything. Here, the light of the room was soft and orange. In the morning, we would hike back up to Darjeeling and a few days later, catch a series of trains back to Calcutta to submit our final report to JSK and see our friends, Sarmishtha and Debasish, one last time.

But on this evening, Sutay and the Nepalese mother of the house exchanged smiles as they talked, and, I, squatting on the earthen floor, held my cup out for more beer.

TWENTY

Bodh Gaya: Unexpected stop

After six months, our time in India was coming to an end—compressing in front of us in the final weeks before our flight date, so that all the amazing things we had seen were coming up against the enormity of the things we had not seen.

We said good-bye to Sarmishtha and Debasish in Calcutta on the platform of Howrah Station, our throat-clenching farewell interrupted by a beggar who kept thrusting his stump into our good-bye hugs. Sutay and I climbed aboard the Rajdhani Express for a three-day, first class rail journey to New Delhi, followed by a flight to Bangkok and the next phase of our trip.

With our remaining time, we could do a whistle-stop tour of must-see sites like Varanasi and the Taj Mahal—or we could try to carve out some time to pause in one place and soak in what we had seen so far.

When I first met Sutay, she had just earned a yoga teacher certification, and I knew it was a dream of hers to do some kind of retreat in India; yet we hadn't made that happen. We were torn on how best to spend the next few weeks, and as we decided, we bought westbound train tickets and climbed on board.

We'd decided to travel in style on our final Indian train ride, after so many months of raw, hockey-snotting, second-class rail experiences. In coach, there had been cockroaches on the walls, grime on the floors, and a stream of pushy beggars sweeping dirt around our feet. On one second-class train, a beggar, through hostile sign language, threatened to spit on me if I didn't cough up some rupees. I threw the coins in his direction while my fellow passengers laughed. And, of course, there were the toilets—horrid, splattered squatters where the tracks passed directly beneath the hole, and there was nothing clean to hold on to as the car rocked back and forth.

Good times.

V.S. Naipaul wrote, "Indian Railways! They are part of the memory of every traveler, in the north, east, west or south.... the shouts of stunted, sweating porters, over-eager in red turbans and tunics, the cries of tea-vendors with their urns and clay cups...."

Once, amid all this stained chaos of a crowded coach car, Sutay and I had to share a single, fold-down berth in a compartment overflowing with extended families. After lights-out, my wife and I battled for space while we listened to the passengers around us snore-fart-burp the night away. Some of the biggest battles of our honeymoon were fought over precious centimeters of sleeping space that night.

But the Rajdhani Express was another story. We had a private sleeper compartment, which we quickly found and occupied. We unloaded our packs and enjoyed a stream of visits by dapper servers with hot soup, tea, and biscuits. When it was time to sleep, to Sutay's delight, an attendant arrived with fresh linens for our berths. It was wonderful and we settled in to enjoy it—until something we read in our guidebook, *Rough Guides India*, caused us to rethink our plans.

We realized we would be rumbling right through the state of Bihar and the village of Bodh Gaya. There, twenty-six hundred years before, a wandering prince named Siddhartha Gautama, sat under a bodhi tree and meditated his way beyond worldly suffering to become the Buddha, the "enlightened one." This event is considered the holiest moment in Buddhism, proving that anybody on this earth has the ability to do the same. The spot where it happened—where a descendant of the actual tree under which he sat, was only a *tuk-tuk* ride from the station in Gaya, which we would be passing around three in the morning.

Sutay and I were rather Buddha-curious at the time, and to discover that we were passing by Bodh Gaya seemed more than serendipitous. It would be like a budding Elvis fan driving across the United States and suddenly realizing he was in front of the gates to Graceland. Would we really blow right by the Place of Enlightenment because we were enjoying the material comforts of a luxury train?

The irony would have been too much. Buddha found this spot after he had left his father's opulent palace, shunning his prince-hood and all material possessions to wander in the wilderness and arrive at this place.

So, in the middle of the night, we gathered our bags and, when the train stopped in Gaya, we said good-bye to our linens and the Rajdhani Express and walked out of the palace gates.

The train disappeared and left us standing in silence among a sea of bodies. There were no touts, no rickshaw drivers pulling at us like there were during the day. Just people sleeping on the platform, rows of them, clusters of them, all lying down, all bathed in the dark of night. It was eerie picking our way through the sleeping figures. We walked and searched, and finally found a rickshaw to Bodh Gaya where we woke up a hotel *wallah* and crashed in a plain, clean room.

We awoke in a hot, dry village of about 30,000 people, both native residents and also many thousands of religious pilgrims from around the world. Despite the Buddhist centerpiece—the sacred tree and temple complex surrounding it—in typical Indian fashion, there was also a loud, vibrant mixture of faiths and cultures on display in the streets and alleys of Bodh Gaya. When we arrived the village was celebrating two overlapping festivals—Eid for the Muslims and Diwali for the Hindus. All night long the village was filled with amplified music, firecrackers, and shouting, but it was happening on a small scale, without the multitudes of people we'd seen in Calcutta and Delhi. Bodh Gaya, noise and all, was an oasis of peace in the thrumming chaos of India.

Still trying to figure out just why we'd decided to stop here, Sutay and I entered the Om Café, a small eatery near a cement apartment building for Tibetan refugees. We ordered *momo* dumplings and yoghurt *lassis* while a sacred Sanskrit mantra,

"Om Mani Padme Hum," played in the background over and over and over.

As I sucked the thick yoghurt drink through my straw, a flyer on the bulletin board above our table caught my attention: "A Journey into Mindfulness," it said. "Join us in a ten-day meditation and yoga retreat, in silence and in motion at the Root Institute for Wisdom Culture."

This was, literally, the sign we'd been waiting for. We couldn't stay in India forever, but perhaps we could delay our departure just a bit. Attending the retreat would mean changing our flight and paying a fee, but perhaps it would be worth it. We finished our plates, ordered more tea, and decided to stay.

TWENTY-ONE

A moment
of silence

The grounds of the Root Institute for Wisdom Culture were
a ten-minute bicycle rickshaw ride from central Bodh Gaya.
This was an international learning and meditation center, surrounded by its own walls and beyond them on all sides, by
dusty, fallow rice fields. The sign at the entrance declared in
red paint:

"No Killing, No Stealing, No Lying, No Sexual Activity,
Dress Appropriately, Let the Monks and Nuns Eat First, No
Music, Dance, Singing, This Is a Meditation Environment."

Inside was a verdant picture of peace, especially compared
to the stark, trash-studded brown landscape around it. The
well-watered grounds were verdant and shaded. A cluster of
dormitories and temples was set amid golden Buddha statues,

water elements, flower beds, and a few wandering goats and puppies for good measure.

Sutay and I were issued separate rooms and told not to speak with each other except during the daily group talks, in which we were encouraged to participate. "There are degrees of silence," one of the monks explained. "There is 'noble silence,' which means no eye contact, no interacting with others, no smiling or looking at each other. But this is not what we're asking. We ask only that you refrain from unnecessary verbal communication."

We knew this was part of the deal, the silence and separation; still, it was strange to go to bed alone that first night in such a plain room, a flashback to my previous solitary life. Remembering those times of longing made what I now had that much more amazing—Sutay in my life, doing what we were doing, staring straight into our future, but first, learning how to be in the present. The security of that was assuring and I fell asleep happy, eager to report to morning class.

————————

The *gompa*, or prayer hall, where we gathered at dawn, was decorated in bright Tibetan style, with reds and golds, woven *thangkas*, and framed photos of various high lamas, including the smiling image of the Dalai Lama.

"The first fruit of meditation is slowing down," said Rita Riniker, a Buddhist monk from Austria who would be our guide for the next ten days. Her robes were scarlet, matching the room.

Eighteen of us were seated on the floor. We were random travelers from a dozen different countries. As we sat and adjusted and squirmed, we heard birds outside, a barking dog, and the droning loudspeaker from an eye clinic that had been set up under circus tents in one of the empty paddies outside the institute walls.

"Sitting here," said Rita, "with the intention of becoming calm and peaceful, is enough."

That was all we had to do. It was that simple. After a few tips on how to balance our bodies, observe our thoughts, and stay awake, Rita began the session as she would every morning for the next ten days. First, the slow, building chime of her prayer bowl, followed by its long, tapering into silence; then she said, "There is nothing to achieve. There is nothing to attain."

One of my legs began going numb; my back ached; a mosquito landed on my ear. This was not going to be easy.

———

Morning meditation began at 5:45 a.m. followed by yoga at 6:30, then breakfast, walking meditation, sitting meditation, a short break, yoga before a veggie lunch, group discussions (the only sanctioned time to speak), break, dharma talks, break, yoga, light dinner, walking meditation, sitting meditation, sleep.

Repeat.

This structure was actually a welcome change after the floating free-fall of the road. The silence was nice too, offering a break from the standard backpacker chatter to which we were accustomed. Karin, a participant from Germany, said during our first group talk how nice the silence was: "You don't have to be anyone or impress anyone, or brag about where you've been and where you're going or how long you've been traveling. We're all just here, the same in silence. There are no stories, no competition, age doesn't matter, background doesn't matter."

But on that first morning, I found both physical and mental barriers to gaining any deep peace of mind. I gritted my teeth against the pain in my calves, my mind flashed from thought to thought with no focus. This was going to take time, I knew. And that was the thing—you had to take the time. I straightened my back and loosened my shoulder blades. My eyes were open, taking in the soft light. *Slow down*, I said to myself. *Slow down, slow downslowdownslowdown.*

I snuck a glance at Sutay across the room, my forbidden lover, perched on her mat like a queen, the straightest posture in class. Still, I wondered how she was doing. It was tough not being able to check in with her.

One morning we broke the rules and met clandestinely atop my dorm at 5 a.m., before the sun rose. We stood on the flat roof and embraced for a long while, not saying anything. Finally, the first hint of red-orange light appeared in the east, behind a distant hundred-foot-tall seated Japanese Buddha statue across several rice fields. We'd visited the site as tourists the week before.

Now Sutay and I were looking at it from a different angle and in a very different light. We whispered quick stories and I made sure she was enjoying it all, then we descended the stairs, one at a time, and made it to the *gompa* before the morning bell.

TWENTY-TWO

The weeping monk

"There will be many people there," Rita had warned us. "But it is quite special to go to such a big, loud place in silence."

It was the final day of our retreat, and we were about to go on our first field trip outside the compound walls. If anyone tried to speak with us, Rita had explained, we should simply place index fingers to our lips and they would understand. This method had worked like a charm earlier that evening, when we'd entered the complex and vendors of lotus flowers, incense, and postcards flocked to us. We calmly did as Rita had instructed and they parted like water.

The Mahabodhi archaeological site and its myriad statues and stupas is a recent discovery, excavated in the 1800s, and its status as a spiritual pilgrimage site (not to mention destination for Western retreat-goers) is newer still. Most of the gleaming multitude of monasteries in Bodh Gaya were built by other nations with Buddhist populations—gilded temples from Japan, Burma, Thailand, and others, each distinct in its national style, each offering basic accommodations for visiting monks who come to pay their respects to the holy bodhi tree.

The tree, a descendant of a cutting that had been spirited away to Sri Lanka when the original tree was chopped down, grows next to an enormous conical stupa. Signs in various languages announced the place's significance from the fences and walls surrounding the tree's intertwined trunks.

The reason for our group trip to the main temple that night was to deliver a set of robes. Each month during the full moon, the Root Institute *sangha*, or community of monks and nuns, places a fresh set of robes on the golden Buddha in the inner sanctum, supposedly at the actual spot where Prince Siddhartha Guatama sat and became enlightened more than two thousand years ago. "Offering robes to the Buddha," Rita had said, "is the perfect gift. It is the only thing he needs."

As participants in the retreat, we were invited to come along and observe, then spend some time outside under the sacred tree. We accepted.

———

Sutay and I ducked into the stupa's sole chamber, silently shouldering our way through a knot of white-robed Koreans and dreadlocked Canadians till we caught up with Rita and our group. We knelt with them before a giant sitting Shakya-muni Buddha. Rita delivered a reading above the din of the visitors as she handed the new robes to the attendant, who replaced the month-old fabric that was there.

All the while, tourists, monks, and vacationing Indian families took turns posing in front of the statue, adding a subtle tension between spiritual sobriety and flash-snapping levity.

When the robes were in place, Sutay and I squeezed back outside. The November air was pleasant, the stone under our bare feet cool. The moon cast shadows behind hundreds of centuries-old icons. After our time inside the retreat walls, the energy of the temple crowd—a thousand chattering and chanting pilgrims from around the world—was not as jarring as I'd expected. A mood of relaxed bustle prevailed, tranquil, filled with purpose.

Monks wore color-coded robes, according to their country and sect, forming a rainbow of maroon, orange, white, and yellow. Some were solitary, others sat in neat rows, reciting group mantras. Others posed for each other's cameras, kneeling, un-smiling, palms joined at their hearts while their companions clicked and flashed away. Pilgrims and tourists blurred.

———

There was not much idle chit-chat beneath the branches of the sacred bodhi tree, so I was surprised when a monk sat down between Sutay and me, leaned over, and asked in nervous English where we were from.

I looked across him at Sutay. Do we really raise a finger to our lips and shush a monk? Wasn't the respectful thing to answer the monk? Especially sitting in such an auspicious place? We were beneath the actual branches of the bodhi tree! I hesitated, trying to get a read from Sutay. I wanted to be polite and respectful, but how could we break our silence right at the moment when the whole week seemed to be coming together?

The branches reached far beyond its enormous, squat fenced-in trunk, creating an extensive canopy under which many people were sitting. To be clear: The bodhi tree is not considered a representation of God; neither is the statue of Buddha that resides inside the stupa, nor the hundreds of images of Buddha scattered throughout the grounds. Buddha is not considered a deity. His enlightenment was no miracle, but an example of what any human being can do by sitting under a tree. The bodhi tree and statues are symbols of how we all have the potential to do the same—that is, escape suffering and be happy.

"America," I heard myself saying. "U.S.A."

I had barely spoken for over a week. My voice sounded strange.

"Thailand," he said, pointing to his chest. "Here, four week." He pointed to his bedroll, indicating that this was the spot where he'd been camping, sleeping under these branches and the stars. Only monks were allowed to sleep inside the temple complex.

Our new friend smiled broadly when he saw that I understood him about where he'd been sleeping. Then he told us he was leaving the next day and his smile disappeared.

Moonlight washed over the leaves and flickering candles and floodlights, incense, and song. We sat on the grass and crossed our legs, facing the tree, watching the sweeping scene before us, reflecting on the internal activity of the past week, then swinging back again to the present moment.

"We must train our naughty mind," Rita had taught us. "We must treat it playfully like a puppy or a small child. If it runs away from you, smile, but bring it back in. If your dog or your child is disciplined, they are not afraid or confused; they know what to do. There is happiness."

After this retreat, I was at least *aware* of my "monkey mind" and could watch it swing in the branches and not let it bother me. I couldn't necessarily stop its shenanigans, but I could slow it for a few moments at a time and for now, this was enough.

I told the monk that we too had been in India for several months and were departing soon, but he didn't understand. He repeated himself, held up his bedroll, and pointed to the spot again. In the next instant, the moon's light broke through a gap in the branches. Silver streams widened on the monk's cheeks. He pointed to the moon, then swept his arm to indicate the stupa, the people, the statuettes behind us, the night sky.

"You are sad to leave," said Sutay.

"I am having tears," he said.

The monk took out two fallen bodhi leaves he had collected during his stay and handed one to each of us. Mine was yellow and insect-eaten between its veins, but its heart shape was intact and the empty space between the exposed veins was delicate and beautiful. Sutay's leaf was solid and perfect. I placed them both between the pages of my journal, then put my hands together in gratitude.

Overcome, the monk turned his head away. Sutay and I, silent once again, stood up, leaving him to his final night beneath the branches of the bodhi tree. We exited the complex, found our shoes, and hailed a bicycle rickshaw back to the institute.

PART III

GHANA

TWENTY-THREE

Kwame
and honey

After India, Sutay and I spent several months backpacking circles around southeast Asia and completing a second volunteer assignment in Sri Lanka, again with an NGO that supported tea workers. Then, to extend our trip and reroute it through Africa, we signed up for a third volunteer assignment with American Jewish World Service Volunteer Corps. This time, they placed us with Planned Parenthood Association of Ghana (PPAG).

We arrived in Accra, the crusty coastal capital of Ghana, nearly one year after we'd first set out. We would be working in the central PPAG office in the western part of Accra. Sutay finally had the clinical position she'd wanted all along—working with nurses, doctors, and patients in the family planning and fertility clinic. I would assist the organization's media co-ordinator and youth group. It was another fine match of our respective skill sets and the needs of a local organization.

More importantly, accepting an assignment in West Africa put us within striking distance of Sutay's Peace Corps village in The Gambia, just a few countries up the coast. Her dream of returning there with a husband in tow was one step closer to reality.

But first, Accra.

At Kotoka International Airport, a driver from PPAG was waiting for us with a sign with our misspelled names on it. No matter, it's always a treat to be greeted at the airport in a strange place! George loaded us into his car, then took us out for fried chicken in the Osu tourist district and answered my newbie questions about currency and culture.

Sutay had been there before, but this was my first time in Africa. Luckily, Ghana was considered a kind of "West Africa 101" for travelers—English-speaking, relatively safe and stable, with a lengthy history of hosting foreign groups, delegations, and travelers.

Once the center of the Ghana and Mali empires, Ghana has been famous at various times throughout its history for its commerce in slaves, gold, and cacao. The Gold Coast, as the region is called, was a British colony until 1957, when Ghana became the first African nation to claim independence. British colonizers left behind their language and a wonderful affinity for dark beer—I vote Castle Milk Stout best beer of the trip.

But history (and beer) aside, when Sutay and I arrived in 2006, the country was all about soccer. Its national team, the Ghana Black Stars, had just qualified for the World Cup for the first time in history. George told us all about it over lunch, then drove us across the city, skirting the ocean, where the smell of the ocean mixed with sewage from Korle Lagoon. The parts of the beach we could see were covered with debris and plastic.

I know the odor of low tide, smoldering trash, and diapers isn't necessarily romantic, but I couldn't help reflecting on all the smells my wife and I had smelled together over the last year, all the stimuli we'd taken in while sitting next to each other in taxis, planes, boats, and rickshaws. We'd moved and adapted together, reacted and rejoiced, and now, driving through downtown Accra with the windows down, we were doing it some more.

George brought us to the fully furnished home of a Ghanaian nurse who was working abroad in London. This is where we would stay, in one of the two bedrooms. Family photos of weddings, communions, and graduations were mixed with Christian paraphernalia on the walls, giving a surreal, voyeuristic feel to our accommodations. The house was comfortable enough, but the whole arrangement was disturbingly emblematic of everything wrong with international aid—i.e., an experienced Ghanaian nurse works abroad in the U.K. (contributing to Ghana's brain drain), while American volunteers occupy her house to work for free in a local clinic. But there we were. Another temporary life had been dropped down around us.

This time we shared our house with four roommates and two dogs. Effo was our main caretaker, a balding, friendly man of about 50; Yaya was the cleaner and cook, a bright, bouncing 26-year-old student; Kojo was Yaya's 15-year-old brother; and his friend, Odartey. The two boys slept on the floor, took orders from Effo and Yaya, called me "Uncle Joshua," and greeted us warmly (eventually with hugs) each day when we returned from the office. Odartey was 14 and very smart. Kojo was not as sharp. Yaya and Effo constantly called him "stupid" and explained to us and other visitors, "There is something wrong with the child," right in front of him. Kojo and Odartey fed, bathed, and sometimes kicked and beat the house's two skinny, tail-wagging dogs, Blackie and Brownie.

"Kwame, how are you?" Effo would greet me each morning. Kwame (rhymes with "swami") was my Ghanaian name. It was given to all men born on Saturday. Sutay was also born on Saturday, so her name was "Ama," but in our house Yaya preferred to call her "Honey" after she heard me do so once. The boys followed suit and the name stuck. We were officially Mr. Kwame Berman and Madame Honey.

Our commute to work was a half-hour urban stroll, while traffic raged in the streets and we dodged goats, taxis, and dogs. Because we walked through the same neighborhood day after day, joining the flow of people, certain vendors started to recognize us along our route and waved, calling us "obruni," or whitey. Sometimes they sold us corn or fruit, which we would bring home to Yaya to prepare for the family.

At the clinic, Sutay was learning and sharing every day. The nurses delighted in trying to teach her words in Ga, and chastised her when she confused them with the Twi phrases she'd learned from Effo in our home. (We never could get the languages straight.) One day, they laughed behind Sutay's back for eight straight hours when her underwear was showing through her scrubs. They waited all day to tell her and I was there when they finally did. I watched my wife turn bright red as a gaggle of her fellow nurses howled and hugged her.

I worked in a small office side by side with a go-getter named Anang, who was a Christian rock musician on the side. My assignment was okay, but it was not as good a match as Sutay's. Actually, it was my fault. My assignment had potential, but my heart wasn't in it. I enjoyed helping the youth group start a blog and I reported some interesting stories with Anang, but mostly I found myself waiting each afternoon for 5 o'clock.

That's when I'd walk over to wait for Sutay outside the clinic. If patients were still there, I'd sit under the mango tree and scribble in my book, or else I'd walk across the street to try out my Twi with George and the other PPAG drivers standing around their vehicles. Then Honey and I would walk home through Mamprobi.

TWENTY-FOUR

Hidden charms

I consider myself an expert at seeking "hidden charms" and that was most of what Ghana had to offer. I appreciated the grimy pluck of Accra. I chose to see its lack of tourist attractions as an opportunity, not a shortcoming, a vacuum that forces you to fine-tune your traveler's antennae and fill it wisely.

You slow down.

On Fridays, Sutay and I often splurged on a night out in Osu, the closest the city had to a tourist district, clear across town. We had to travel there via a string of *tro-tros* and taxis. It was an undertaking. To avoid the traffic, our drivers chose exotic back-alley shortcuts. Taxi windows, in addition to letting in foul air, framed a thousand images, scenes, and stories of this city.

It was worth it to meet up with other expats and volunteers for sidewalk beers, Italian food, Lebanese *meze*, and roast chicken. There were bookstores in Osu, plus Frankie's Bakery and vendors selling beads, drums, and soccer jerseys. It was exciting compared to our neighborhood in Mamprobi.

Between outings to the fun side of town, we droned along in a nine-to-five existence. Accra was a hot, in-your-face city. The simple act of walking on the roads or getting into a public bus was an ordeal. The weeks wore on. A couple of times, I woke up not remembering what country I was in, sorting quickly through an inventory of beds and memories before I figured it out. I started to dwell on the next chapter ahead of us. I was ready, I felt, to get home and get on with things. I was tired.

It was difficult to explain, even to Sutay, who had never seen me mope before. Another part of it was not seeing the forest for the trees—the trip of a lifetime stretched behind and before us, making it difficult to see the scope of the thing, we were so deep inside it.

———————

One Sunday morning, the day spread before me like a swamp, thick with heat, white with light even in the porch's shade; the day was as empty as the gray sky. As I approached the bitter, black dregs at the bottom of my coffee cup, I felt far away. Which is where I was, far away in an unremarkable neighborhood of an unremarkable African capital, with nothing to do, nowhere to go. I'd finished reading my fifth novel in a month and hadn't the heart to pick up another, ashamed at being in such an exotic locale and wanting only to escape in stories.

So I sat and listened to the soundscape of our neighborhood over the glass-topped walls of our fence.

"Eh-mo eyyy!" shouted the fish seller. "I have fish!" I recognized her voice. We passed her every weekday morning as we walked to Blacksmith Junction to catch our bus. She had an enormous tin tub on her head, overflowing with silver-black, empty-eyed fish, arranged in circular rows.

"Eh-mo eyyy!" Her voice carried for blocks, approaching, growing louder as I sat, stopping when customers approached to buy something. Across the street, drums throbbed from the Pentecostal church, and the shouting and singing were growing in intensity. I wished I had some such outlet or the energy to get up and walk into an unexplored section of this city. Instead, I walked inside the house, past Yaya, Effo, Kojo, and Odartey, all zombied out to another soccer match on TV in the stifling heat of the living room. I poured a glass of water and went back to the porch.

Sutay was still asleep. I sat back down, sipped my water, and kept listening. Things were picking up in the church, the drums getting louder, with the occasional "Jesus" and "Amen" ringing through the songs and chants in Twi.

I tried to be in the moment, tried not to look ahead at the months, the years, the lifetime(!) before us. Sutay saw our near-future clearly. She knew what lay ahead—bills, loans, jobs followed by births, babies, and diapers. We wanted all these things and knew what we were getting into, but in general, Sutay dreaded our return and would have gladly kept extending our trip, at least till the money was gone, which was not far off anyway.

In the church, orderly rhythms were breaking down into chaotic shouts, some tribal version of holy-roller cousins across the ocean in West Virginia. Odartey came out on the porch and I asked him what they were singing.

"'We are alive,'" he said. "They are saying, 'We are not dead—by the holy spirits we are alive.'"

Accra was alive all right. I sometimes tasted it, urban dust, metallic on my tongue; sometimes felt its sting in my eyes.

"We need to get out of this city," I said to Sutay when she finally got up and joined me on the porch. As my people say, from my mouth to God's ears. The next morning when we arrived at the office, our supervisor told us she needed someone to deliver some materials to a rural PPAG outpost in the north, which she thought we might want to see.

"You can stay at the clinic there," she said. "Would you like to go?"

"Yes!" we said.

"You'll have to take the bus on your own," she said, "first to Kumasi, then to Tamale."

"Okay," said Sutay.

"Alhaji Mammah Tenii will meet you in Tamale. He will take you to Kparigu, where you will meet Chief and the midwives."

It was perfect. We had a mission, a reason to travel. I felt my spirits lifting at the thought of the unknown ground before us. Jobs, mortgage, car insurance, and HOA meetings were still in our impossible future. Right now, we had a rendezvous in Tamale.

"Mammah will arrange everything," said our supervisor.

TWENTY-FIVE

Ghana will always win

We arrived at the bus station in Accra before the sun was up, early enough to get a decent spot in the line that had already formed at the bus door. We high-fived each other as we sank into our seats for the next eight hours, the first phase of a two-day trip to Tamale.

Finally, an hour late, the driver boarded the bus and greeted everyone as he stood in the aisle. He wore a loose, knee-length, blue smock over dark pants and polished shoes. He faced everybody and spoke in a loud voice. "We are about to begin our journey to Kumasi. May God be with us all."

Everybody on the bus responded on cue with an "Amen!"

Of all our travels, Ghana was probably the most outwardly Christian place we'd been to. You need only look at the names of small businesses along the streets of Accra. I tried to scribble down as many as I could: "By His Grace Beauty Salon," "God Lives Cement House," "Jesus Is Alive Boutique." The list is long.

We lurched into morning traffic. The driver took our vehicle through crazy backstreet detours to avoid the morning gridlock. He blared the radio, a morning talk show whose topic was, of course, the Ghana Black Stars and the upcoming World Cup tournament. It was a historical moment for Ghana, and the country was on fire about it. During games, all of Ghana shut down to watch. I read that the government ordered several industrial and gold-mining operations to cease so there would be electricity for everyone's televisions.

In addition to the Black Stars, four other African teams had qualified for the final tournament in Germany. Africa pride was in the air, and Black Star mania reigned during our time there. Our housemates, Yaya, Effo, Kojo, and Odartey, dominated the television outside our bedroom, watching every game, whether Ghana was playing or not, and singing the national anthem at every commercial:

> Raise high the flag of Ghana,
> And one with Africa advance,
> Black Star of hope and honor,
> To all who thirst for liberty!

Team jerseys were on sale on every street corner in Accra with the names and numbers of the stars: Mensah, Appiah, Amoah, Essien, Kingson. The excitement continued to build, peaking one day with Ghana's match against the United States.

In Mamprobi, the neighborhood where we lived, each of Ghana's goals against the United States was followed by an eruption of people into the streets—entire families playing drums, singing, shaking gourds, shouting. When the game was over, Ghana had won 2–1, defeating the United States!

Sutay and I raced out of our gates with Effo, Yaya, and the boys to join mobs of young and old in the streets. People drag-raced cars down the street, shirtless men hanging out of the car windows (we pressed our backs to the fence when they passed); other groups ran wild with flags, chanting, singing, shouting: "Ghana besha debiya!" Ghana will always win!

People climbed atop vehicles to dance and formed im-promptu processions of celebrants. I paraded through the streets with a group of teens. They draped me with yellow-red-and-green flags and shouted over and over, "Don't cry, *obruni*! Don't cry!"

I congratulated everyone I met. I said, "You scored my coun-try!" This was their way of saying "defeated." I laughed at their taunts, then asked if I could take their picture. When I re-turned to our house, spent and sweaty, covered with dust, Effo sent Kojo, one of the boys, down the block for a basket of beers. We sat in front of the house with our neighbor, Uncle John, whose granddaughters danced around us, and we shouted to whoever passed, "Ghana besha debiya!"

On the packed bus that morning, traveling across the city, everyone listened attentively to *The Choice Breakfast Show* on Joy FM. Beating the United States was one thing, but in the next round, the Black Stars faced Brazil, five-time World Cup champs and the top-rated team in the world. No matter.

Ghanaians were riding so high on their team's Cinderella trajectory—the only African team to advance this far in the World Cup ever!—that they started having wild delusions of success.

The DJ was taking callers who were divided into fatalists who saw no chance of beating Brazil, and believers—the minority—who thought there was some hope.

"If you fight a lion and die, it is better than fighting a dog!" said one caller.

"Let us call for a national hour of prayer," said the next caller. "God will make sure we win. The Almighty will provide. Tomorrow we will know if God is fair or if He is not fair."

Others made predictions: "Brazil–1, Ghana–0!"

"Why?" the DJ asked.

"The Black Stars brought their girlfriends with them to Germany, so how can they perform? These boys do not control themselves! If you touch a woman, it takes seven days to recover before a game. That is football! Self-control! Argentina, Brazil, and the U.K. have learned this!"

As we approached the edge of Accra, the DJ was on a roll. "What does Brazil have?" he asked. "They have the samba! Where did the samba come from? From Africa! Brazilian voodoo princes put pins in Black Star dolls' faces, yes! But whatever Brazil has, we have better!"

The bus burst into applause and shouts of approval.

"Are Brazilians not human?" he continued. "Then can we not *score* them? Let us pray."

"Amen!" shouted several passengers.

As we left the city limits and pointed due north into the interior, the radio began breaking up, turned to static, then was drowned by the breeze, which was finally moving through the bus and drying the sweat on our foreheads.

———————

The next day, the second leg of the trip began early in the dark on the patio of our Kumasi hotel. I'd slept like a rock to the crickets purring in the tall grass behind our room and was excited to move farther into the country. We ate omelets, drank instant coffee, and watched a replay of a news reporter interviewing a few of the Black Stars on TV. Today was game day, Ghana v. Brazil, David confronting another Goliath in a massive German arena with the whole world watching.

Sutay and I walked to the station and waited for the bus to show. We boarded, waited as the driver prayed in both Twi and English, joined the choral "Amen!" then pulled away, two hours behind schedule. This ensured that everyone on the bus would miss at least the first quarter of the game, and I heard people grumbling about it.

Seven hours later, a wide, round-faced man named Mammah met us in Tamale and took us to the Catholic Guesthouse where he had arranged a simple room with a private bathroom for us. We joined staff and guests clustered around a single, tiny television in the dining room. Ghana was down one point. That they had been robbed of the last goal was the consensus. The referee was racist! This was not fair!

When Ghana lost, denial quickly turned into a surge of support for the Black Stars. A parade of bodies entered the streets, shouting, drumming, and chanting. After two days on a bus, I wanted to walk. Sutay wasn't feeling well and stayed in the room while I walked across town with the celebrants, past the mosque, its silhouette against orange light, through the market, and back in the dark.

I woke Sutay and told her she had to eat and drink something. I'd watched her appetite fade all day and knew she needed something. I brought dinner from the kitchen—rice, guinea fowl, and red sauce, but she barely touched it before going back to sleep.

I turned off the light to join her, each of us in a single bed with no mosquito nets. The first bites came just as I drifted off, on my shoulders. They morphed into rounded domes, the tops of mosques, mosquitoes that invited me inside, rounded backs but with flat fronts, bites and dreams, tossing and turning.

I awoke to realize it was only midnight. The fan had stopped, the power was out, and I was going to drip sweat through the night with no hope of blowing the bugs away. I heard Sutay struggling to sleep in her creaking bed across the room. The night dragged on until the sky at last lightened. In less than hour Mammah would take us to his office, where we'd meet the mysterious Chief. I rose to enter this wide-open moment in north Ghana. I tried the shower, nothing more than a tepid trickle of water, but enough to distract me from the bites and exhaustion and itching.

TWENTY-SIX

Taking fufu with Chief

Chief David Kansuk Laari entered Mammah Tenii's office wearing a traditional striped, knee-length smock and matching cotton hat. He was a giant of a man in many ways, starting with his physical presence and continuing with his jobs: He was both chief medical assistant for Planned Parenthood Association of Ghana's Northern Region and Chief of Nakpanduri, a position in the Ghanaian government, which mixed tribal chieftaincy with elected officialdom.

Chief held out his hand and declared that we would leave for Kparigu with him the following morning, not this afternoon as we'd planned. First, he had to buy supplies for the clinic, pay bills, and visit one of his wives. "Would you like to accompany me?" he asked.

Sutay was still feeling under the weather, but didn't appear too sick. After a brief consult, Chief advised her to rest. She happily lay back down on the couch in Mammah's air-conditioned office. While she rested, they would talk about family and fertility issues for hours and also about PPAG's work in the area. There was no doubt some deep nostalgia mixed with Sutay's nausea—to be back in Africa discussing public health issues with local experts, just like in the old days.

I took off with Chief and his driver, Baba, to head into central Tamale. Chief made his rounds, totally involved with the details of his various business deals, checking lists, presiding over the packing and tying of supplies to the truck. We picked up drugs and medical supplies from several pharmacies, then went to a giant warehouse and waited around until the sacks of fertilizer he'd ordered were ready—for his family farm next to the clinic.

As we drove around or waited for deliveries, I asked Chief Kansuk about his life and he was happy to answer.

"I was born in 1954," he said. "My mother's name was Borika, which means 'there is no hiding place.' My father, Kansuk, had nine wives, each with one child in school and one on the farm."

In 1964, David was taken out of school because his mother's co-wives were jealous of his success. After two years, Borika sent him back to school. Kansuk was furious that his wife had disobeyed him. He cut all relations with her, giving her no food but allowing her to stay in his compound. She kept David in school anyway.

"So I farmed to feed my mother," he said, "I woke at 5 in the morning to tend the crops, then took a bath and went to school. Life was very difficult, especially in the lean season. In

1968 I passed my high school exam, but my father still did not support me. In 1971 I worked as ward assistant at Nalerigu Hospital. In 1973 I moved to Bawku Presby Hospital, where I received my nurse training."

"Did your father ever support you?" I asked.

"In 1975 I saw my father before he died. He was surrounded by his women and his head lay in his senior wife's lap. My father gave me his final advice: 'Be aware of the way you talk. Stay clear of people's matters. Keep your books.'"

So absorbed was Chief in telling me his story, and in the details of his errands, and so hesitant was I to whine about being hungry, that the subject of lunch did not come up until four in the afternoon. My stomach gurgled as we loaded up the last boxes of gloves, bandages, and pills.

"Have you taken *fufu* yet?" Chief asked.

Most Ghanaian meals included a mashed starch—some sticky, dense paste of cornmeal, cassava, or plantain. I avoided most forms of the stuff.

"No," I said. "I've tried *kenke*, but not *fufu*."

"Today you will try *fufu*," he said.

Baba dropped us off near the bus station where Chief and one of his sons led me through a garbage-strewn alley until we came out into a small opening with a few plastic tables and chairs, the scene framed by rusted tin and scrambling chickens and children. We sat down in the middle of this mini-bazaar. A handful of shops, boiling cauldrons, and shoeshine kids occupied the lot. Chief barked an order to a cook tending a nearby open kitchen. Even reclining on his elbows, he was tall and imposing, with a royal, rectangular jawbone and confident frame.

It was a medieval scene. Flies swarmed as they do in such places. Gray wastewater ran in a trench beside us and a boy brought us bowls sloshing with broth before we had landed in our chairs. Gray fist-sized hunks of fatty cow flesh bulged above brown liquid. Next to this was a small plate with a ball of soft, doughy fermented *fufu*.

I pinched off a piece, dipped it in the gravy, and put it in my mouth. It was sour and tangy, and my eyes wandered to the fly-encrusted cauldron from which my gruel had been ladled. In the time it took me to take a few careful, tentative tastes, Chief and his son had devoured half of the meat, gristle, and *fufu*. The next thing I knew, their bowls were rising above upturned faces, and leather-colored streams of soup dripped from their chins to the ground. Not a drop landed on Chief's smock.

Chief looked at my full bowl and gave a laugh and slap on my back. Then he paid the cook while I took a few hearty bites to prove my manhood before getting up to leave.

TWENTY-SEVEN

At the clinic
in Kparigu

Kparigu in northern Ghana is a small settlement of a couple hundred families, mainly Mamprole-speaking farmers plus a few thousand more in the surrounding plains. It has three market days each week, which are the only days public transport is available in and out of town.

The health clinic in Kparigu was built in 1998 by Planned Parenthood Association of Ghana in the style of a rural West African family compound, only each structure is constructed of cement and tin rather than mud and thatch. The walled-in circle of round huts and one rectangular ward of a dozen beds surround a central courtyard, reception window, and medicine dispensary.

The nurses, Ayishetu Yakubu and Auntie Amina, manage the reception area. Patients sign their names on a list in the shaded central area, then sit on the benches until Chief calls them into his consulting room.

Ayishetu, or Sister Ayi, is a tall, formidable woman whose parents had migrated to Ghana from Togo before she was born. She has wide shoulders, a tight bun of hair wrapped in loud colors, a powerful frame, and massive, caring hands that had received many a baby into this world. Auntie Amina (Baba's wife) is shorter, more serious, but just as strong and outgoing.

The night we arrived in the village, Baba and Auntie led us to our quarters behind the clinic, a tiny, oven-hot concrete box of a house. A Peace Corps volunteer named Jessica had once lived there. We entered the super-heated darkness to a narrow, low-hung bed. We thanked our guides, said goodnight, then struggled to hang the mosquito net we'd bought in Accra.

We settled onto the mattress the best we could. In order to fit, we had to sleep head-to-toe, the first time since that Indian train berth nine months before. I lay down, dreading the long, sweat-pooling night ahead of us. It was hard to feel sorry for ourselves, though. We would be here for only a few days, whereas Jessica had lived here for two years. (On our last day Baba would belatedly inform us that Jessica usually slept on a cot in front of his hut with him and his family, under the stars, to keep cool.)

Sister Ayi and Auntie Amina lived in houses adjoining ours, Ayi by herself and Auntie with Baba and their 6-month-old baby girl, Ipti (it means "smile," Auntie told us). Chief's house was a hundred meters away, across his field, down a skinny trail.

Ayi and Auntie were our main guides and caretakers in Kparigu, while Chief was more like a father figure who allowed us to observe him and stepped in for such important things as visiting local leaders.

During the clinic's weekly prenatal day, they worked with Sutay to feel for the position of the fetus and listen to its heartbeat—without machines or monitors. This was how Sutay had originally learned about pregnancy, before she became a registered nurse—as a Peace Corps volunteer herself in The Gambia. They placed their hands on one pregnant belly after another while I photographed them and took notes. After nearly a decade of being away, Sutay was clearly happy to return to the roots of her work, and this made her especially radiant.

One day Ayi was bouncing Ipti on her knee.

"In the West you . . . *push* the baby?" she asked, making the universal stroller-pushing sign.

"Many people do, yes," said Sutay. "But I want to tie mine to me when I have a baby."

Without warning, Ayi ordered my wife to bend forward, then, in what looked like one fluid motion, threw little Ipti on Sutay's back, draped a cloth around them both, and tied it in place. Auntie Amina, Ipti's mother, was watching, along with a few other women, all of whom began to giggle.

Sutay kept one hand behind her, underneath the baby's sprawled legs, until she felt Ipti was not going to fall. Then, in some instinctive mothering reflex, she relaxed and walked forward in a funky little bounce, prompting Auntie and Ayi to howl and double over with laughter. Sutay hammed it up for them, turning the bounce into a kind of dance as Ipti lived up to her name and took to her *obruni* mother with a large grin and excited swats of her hands. This threw the women into hysterics.

"Let's go to the market," said Sister Ayi.

"Yes, it is time!" said Auntie, gesturing to Sutay to keep the baby on her back. They were acting mischievously, as if they knew what a spectacle a white woman with a local baby on her back would cause at the market, and they relished it.

"Let's go," I said.

A few massive trees at the sole crossroads in the village provided shade for the dirt and a handful of merchants. As we arrived, the entire crowd of a hundred or so shoppers and vendors enclosed us in a circle to get a better look.

Mini-mobs gathered round Sutay. Sister Ayi and Auntie Amina played crowd control, barking orders as we waded through the pressing people. Women asked if that was Sutay's baby and Auntie answered, "Of course it is," later laughing and laughing about the looks they'd gotten.

Patients traveled great distances to reach the clinic in Kparigu—walking, bicycling, riding mules or motorcycles from one of the surrounding villages. On the day we observed Chief, most of the patients were children, ablaze with fever. Critical cases, he told us, were referred to the Baptist Hospital in Nalerigu, a rough, ninety-minute drive.

Sutay and I sat in chairs next to Chief, where he commanded from behind his desk, stethoscope around the collar of his bright yellow golf shirt. He placed one massive hand around his patient's skinny arm while with his other hand he made notes in his ledger.

"The child has malaria," he said to us. "She is burning."

"What will you give her?" Sutay asked.

"Chloroquine," he said. He injected the girl's bottom, eliciting a sharp scream and burst of energy, which was quickly exhausted. Chief sent the mother and daughter outside, speaking sharply and pointing them to the outdoor spigot, where the child was to be given a sponge bath, then taken to the ward to rest. Auntie Amina received them, laying the limp, hot, rag doll of a girl onto a sheetless cot.

"This is the beginning of the rainy season," Chief told us. "When it peaks, this clinic sees eighty malaria patients a day."

A motorcycle approached. There were shouts. Chief jumped up to receive a child, eyes rolled into his head, in the middle of a seizure. He called Sister Ayi to bring Valium, which he squirted into the naked child's rectum. The child went limp in Chief's arms. Chief handed the boy back to his father.

"Take the child to the spigot and bathe him," he said. "Then bring him to the ward."

This is how it went the rest of the morning, and for the next three days.

TWENTY-EIGHT

Discussing witchcraft with the Naba of Kparigu

On our third day in Kparigu, the Naba, or village leader, summoned us to his compound. We had been waiting for this, our official welcome, and I'd prepared by stocking up on kola nuts, the traditional gift in West Africa (like bringing a bottle of wine to dinner in Western culture).

"He who brings kola brings life!" Sister Ayi had told me the previous day in the market, helping me to assess the chestnut-like nuts in their piles on the ground. They were grouped by size, color, and quality. I asked for the best.

We reported to Chief Kansuk and followed him to the vehicle. He would accompany us to translate and to explain our presence

in Kparigu, i.e., to observe and help out at the health clinic.
Baba prepared the truck while Chief also inspected the size and
quality of my kola nuts. He approved. We got in the car and
slowly drove a half-mile or so through the dusty village, passing
the crossroads where the market had been and was now empty.

We pulled up in front of the Kpar-Naba's mud-walled complex and walked into a ring of squat, round structures, toward
the center hut. Everything was the color of earth. We lowered
our heads and stepped into the structure's cool shade.

A slight man sat cross-legged, back straight on a floor-level
throne of goat skins. A beaded scepter, cell phone, and motorcycle keys lay on the ground before him. Sutay, Chief, and I sat
on plastic chairs along the wall to the Kpar-Naba's left while
his sons, advisors, and Baba lounged on the ground before him.
A small goat stood unsteadily, a cord around its neck, held by
a boy barely bigger than the animal.

The Kpar-Naba was all smiles, a scrappy goatee hanging
from his pointy chin. He wore a thigh-length, flared smock
and had a variety of hats on the floor at his side, three differ-
ently patterned, different-length cloth hats. He switched head
gear several times during our interview.

"What country?" began the Kpar-Naba, speaking in
Mamprole.

"America," Sutay answered. "U.S.A."

"You came to my village from the U.S.A! Will you take me
back to be Chief there?"

He rocked back with laughter, cracking himself up and
breaking the ice as we laughed with him. I took out the kola
nuts and handed them over. He was pleased. He passed one
of the nuts back to me, which I bit. Its bitterness seized my
tongue and a red strand of saliva dripped onto my notebook.
I chewed.

"Tell me this," said the Kpar-Naba through Chief. "America is so civilized. Why is America so much more civilized than Africa?"

"America," said Sutay, "is advanced in technology, but Africa is advanced in other things."

"What things?" he asked.

"Respect for elders, for one," she said. "Africans are more civilized in this."

Chief translated for him and the Kpar-Naba nodded. "We may not have advanced technology," he said, "but we have 'African electronics'!"

He smiled. I felt like I was missing the joke.

"I can see you all the way in Accra from right here in Kparigu village. I can cause you evil, harm you, set you on fire—and you cannot explain it!"

"He's talking about *juju*," Chief explained as an aside. Sutay stood up without saying a word and slowly lifted the bottom of her shirt. I had no idea what she was doing until she revealed a string of leather-sewn cowrie shells around her waist. It was a charm she'd been given ten years before by a *marabout*, or wandering medicine man, in The Gambia.

"For protection," the Kpar-Naba said, respectfully.

"Yes," she answered. The Kpar-Naba's eyes widened as he realized here was someone—an *obruni* woman, no less!—who shared his passion for "African electronics." He ordered one of his sons to bring his bag of talismans.

It's not that Sutay is a believer in African black magic—or a nonbeliever. She tried to explain it to me once. During her time living in rural Gambia she had seen things that could not be explained. To be safe, she'd kept all the *jujus* she'd received there, including the bone-and-leather charms in the bottoms of our backpacks and the shells around her waist.

"In Africa we have many mysterious things," Chief said.

"I've seen them," said Sutay.

"I'll show you something," said the Kpar-Naba. He held up a cotton smock from the sack. "It is bulletproof. You can touch it."

We reached over and touched it. After feeling the soft material, he made us each touch the bullet lodged beneath the skin of his left knee. The story behind the bullet was lost, though, and when I asked him to clarify, he responded, "I cannot reveal all my secrets! Even between husband and wife there are secrets. Otherwise we Africans become defenseless. We don't have bombs and tear gas," he added, "but we control natural forces, like swarms of bees."

The Kpar-Naba was on a roll. He had something else to show us: a polished stick with a rope wrapped around it. He brought it out with great pride. "This can tie up your entire family. It can kill you in fifteen minutes if you are wrapped in it. It can tie villages, leaders."

The Kpar-Naba stared at Sutay and said, "You can tie down your husband's professional rivals so he will excel in his field."

I tried not to snicker at the image of my fellow travel writers tied up mysteriously at their desks, fingers paralyzed from typing and meeting their deadlines....

"Why did you not use these powers against Brazil?" I asked him. The national Brazilian soccer team had just defeated the Ghana Black Stars, knocking the last African footballers out of the World Cup. The Kpar-Naba laughed and said that Germany, where the 2006 tournament was held, was too far away, too much distance to assist the Black Starts in their final World Cup match.

Then Sutay told a story from The Gambia. She was coaching a soccer team of youths from her village, and in their first game in another village, the boys on her team kept falling every time they approached the ball. They could not get close to the ball without face-planting in the dirt. The other team won. The Kpar-Naba and Chief nodded knowingly. It was a *juju* cast by the opposing team's *marabout*, they agreed.

The Kpar-Naba shifted on his skins. One finger twirled the goat fur by his feet as he listened, the other reached out and squished a bug against the ground. He decided something, then reached into a bowl behind him and handed Sutay a double handful of eggs. "These are guinea fowl eggs. Eat them so the blood of your firstborn son will be strong."

Sutay's eyes met mine as she opened her hands and accepted the eggs. We had visited a few fertility shrines during our travels, and Sutay had purchased some pot-bellied African dolls to help adorn our path to familyhood, but this was perhaps the most pointed blessing for children (a "son," anyway) that we had yet received.

The Kpar-Naba's boy then handed me the goat's leash.

"He is giving you the goat," said Chief, "to make light soup."

A woman appeared and placed two bowls of food before the Kpar-Naba. It was our cue to leave. A long string of good-byes and welcomes and thank-yous trailed us out of the hut as we left him to his lunch. As I filed past him, he was dipping sticky lumps of *fufu* into a bowl of gravy.

I rode in the back of the pickup with our new goat while Sutay, cradling the small, hard-shelled eggs in her lap, rode inside with Chief.

Chief's cell phone rang as we arrived at the clinic. It was his wife in Nakpanduri, his home village. We watched him nod several times before hanging up. "Someone has killed a sacred crocodile and is refusing to pay the fine."

"Why did they call you?" I asked.

"The elders were unable to resolve the matter. You will come to Nakpanduri as my guests. Be ready in one hour."

TWENTY-NINE

The case of the crocodile killer

"In that river," said Chief, in his clear, booming voice, "you cannot kill even a *fish*. That river, it is a god. The fine for the man who did this was two fowl—one white and one of mixed colors—and a sheep. This punishment was passed by the elders, not me. To pacify god."

Chief sat shotgun, Sutay and I were in the backseat, and Baba drove. We had just spent several days watching Chief in his white lab coat, stethoscope, and thick glasses. Now we would see him don his robes and a crown.

As we left Kparigu and entered Chief's territory, we watched him morph from trained medical assistant to traditional village leader. In the Nalerigu market, men and women kneeled when they recognized who was in the passenger seat, and he waved through the open window. The people bowed their heads and clapped their hands slowly and loudly, a salute as we passed.

"What do the people expect you to do about the crocodile?" I asked.

"Hold a trial, look at the evidence. Then the man will be fined and punished for disobeying the elders. We must make an example," Chief explained. "The crocodile will be buried, purified, the gods appeased by judgment so no harm will come to the village."

Shelling peanuts on top of his briefcase, Chief stayed in the car with Sutay, while Baba and I went shopping for tomatoes, rice, onions, and bananas—gifts for Chief's wives who would be cooking for us that evening.

When we were all back in the car and traveling again, I asked Chief, "Are you Christian or Muslim?"

"Christian," he replied. "My father went to church every Christmas. I go to church on Sundays when I can. But there is no pastor in Kparigu. So I preach to the people."

"So you're a medical assistant, a nurse, a village chieftain, a judge, *and* a preacher?" I asked.

He smiled. "It is challenging," Chief said after a pause. "I am caught between my position at the clinic and exercising my role as Chief. But they help each other too."

"How?"

"Being Chief helps me probe further with patients, ask questions, get to the heart of the issue. Most Western doctors do not have time to do this. Kparigu is a violent town. Nurses have been chased out of that community. There are no police. The people are suspicious. They told us our clinic would not succeed. But I knew how to talk to the Kpar-Naba and five years later . . . we are still there."

"How did you become Chief?" asked Sutay.

"It was a fight," he answered. "One is not born a Chief, one has to fight hard for it, but in my case it was also meant to be."

Village leaders sit on piles of hides and cushions, he explained. To be "on the skins" means to be in office, in power. Chief was the Naba of Nakpanduri, but his skin name was Na-Golbilla, which means "Small Moon."

"When the moon comes out," he said, "people are happy, there is light about the place, children are playing."

"How many children do you have," Sutay asked.

"Thirteen," he said, "Caesar, Ferdinand, Ferguson, Felix, Roland, Nagamni, Jeremiah, and Kennedy are the boys. The girls are Gertrude—she's a teacher, her name is Ypnumi which means 'God knows'—Patience, Bidibiya, and Christiana."

"How many wives do you have?"

"Three," he said. "My father had nine. This is what my people expect. My first wife I married because her father predicted I would be the next Chief."

"And your second wife?" Sutay asked.

"When I was taking the chieftaincy, I was only 40 years old. I was the youngest Chief ever to be considered in the history of my village. This caused many problems. Even though it was my family's turn to provide a Chief, there was this dispute over my age. 'He's a small boy and has only one wife,' they said about me. 'I will not bow and clap before a small boy.' It was a big fight and I made my case with the King in Nareligu and with the government in Accra. I took my second wife to legitimize my claim."

_____

In Nakpanduri, as we dropped Chief off in his compound before heading to the guesthouse, he invited us to return later to watch the World Cup football match that evening. Ghana's Black Stars had been ousted from the tournament earlier that week, but Chief was an addict of the sport, he said, and France was playing Brazil, the team that had defeated Ghana. "There is vengeance to be had!" he said.

We returned a few hours later and Chief ordered the television carried into the open-air, dirt-floor courtyard of his palace. Some of his children arranged animal skins and leather pillows on a slab of raised concrete, which served as a throne. There he sat—above his clan and guests, under the stars and a crescent moon.

Sutay beamed to be there, reliving old experiences through my newbie eyes and through the whole unique lens of northern Ghana. It was new for both of us, but we had to sit there and pretend this was normal.

"Kwame!" he shouted to me, "Do you take beer?"

He clapped at a son, handed him a wad of bills, and sent him running for refreshments. Then Chief summoned the local Peace Corps volunteer. Carl—everyone pronounced it "Ka"—was a Minnesotan engineer turned math teacher.

Ka arrived speaking Mwar, the local tongue. He kneeled to clap and sing the proper greetings before Chief. He rose when Chief signaled him to do so, and then Chief greeted him warmly, as a friend.

There's something about seeing a volunteer, deep in his service —totally in his element, his moment—that inspires. Since serving my two years in rural Nicaragua, I always seek active volunteers during my travels. When I was a guidebook author, researching remote regions of Central America, I would find foreign volunteers—whether Peace Corps, British VSO, or other volunteers. They were always willing to share information about where to sleep, eat, or get handmade cowboy boots made. But stumbling across volunteers in the field was also about solidarity and companionship.

Ka excitedly told Chief about the shipment of a hundred bicycles he'd just received. He was in high spirits. He told me and Sutay he'd "hit the jackpot" with his site assignment and we were happy for him and told him so. He enjoyed his teaching, was pumped about the bikes, and there we all were—watching sports on TV under the stars.

Chief ordered more beers to celebrate and maltas, carbonated malt beverages, for Ka's friends from the village who didn't want alcohol.

"What are you? Women?" Chief said to them with a laugh.

After the party (France beat Brazil, 1–0, so we were all happy), Baba drove us back to our room in Nakpanduri's sole guesthouse. It was dark, located atop a raised escarpment, a vegetated ridge snaking away from the village. Built in 1962 for Ghana's founding father, Kwame Nkrumah, the guesthouse had been completed only three weeks before his planned visit. Five years after Ghana declared independence from Great Britain, the president was on his way to the oft-neglected northern parts of the country.

"That morning in the village, all the schoolchildren assembled," Chief said. "We stood there from the early morning with our flags."

But while visiting the Burkina Faso border, Nkrumah was injured by a child who unknowingly carried a bomb in a bouquet of flowers. Nkrumah was flown back to the capital; he survived the blast but never slept in the guesthouse. Tonight, we would sleep in the bed that had been built originally for him and carried all the way to Nakpanduri from the coast.

When we arrived, our presidential suite looked like it hadn't been cleaned since 1962, with stained walls and dirty corners. We crept cautiously under the mosquito net and into the silk sleeping sacks we'd had custom-made in Pakistan, and fell asleep without incident.

———

The following morning Baba delivered breakfast from Chief's compound—a thermos of tea, a few slices of bread, a can of condensed Nestlé milk, and fresh-squeezed orange juice. Sutay and I ate outside next to the garden, then drove down the hill for the big trial.

The courtroom was an outdoor affair, a shade structure of skinny beams, casting bars of light across the scene. Chief sat on a raised dais next to his mother, the only woman there besides Sutay. He wore a long cotton robe with shimmering black, gold, and white stripes; he had on a round, black cap and brown leather shoes. Five or six elders lounged around his feet on the stairs. The elders also wore hats, from Chicago Bulls ski hats to knitted traditional skull caps.

Chief's hungover brother, Bartholomew, was appointed to be my royal, red-eyed interpreter. Chief sat, leaning forward, and listened, chin on hand. He was patient. On the edges of the scene were running children, sleeping dogs, goats, chickens, and pigs.

The accused was a small, hunched old man with a red and white cap and droopy jowls. He said he'd shot at a bird, not a crocodile. Bartholomew breathed stale gin and sweat into my face while explaining the proceedings and translating the lengthy testimonies of the witnesses and the accused, and also Chief's and the elders' responses.

"But you left your sandals there!" thundered Chief, laying out the damning evidence. Chief explained to him how a small community is—"If you cough, everyone knows it."

Chief turned stern, using many slow, dramatic pauses filled only by distant thunder and Bartholomew's booze-stink whispering in my ear.

"I have witnesses prepared to testify that they saw the crime, but I want to avoid disgracing you. Admit to your crime and the punishment will be less. You could have avoided disgrace by admitting and apologizing."

The thunder drew closer, and a storm opened on top of us and everyone moved into a close-aired round hut. When things began again, the accused man's sons shouted, trying to argue and speak for their father, who, during a sudden moment of silence, hissed to Chief, "Bring out your witnesses so I can know my enemies."

It dragged on from there. In the end, Chief fined the man some more cash and "three fowl." The guilty man's face was unmoved, but he made an angry swipe with his hand as he got up to leave. Justice was served.

PART IV

THE GAMBIA

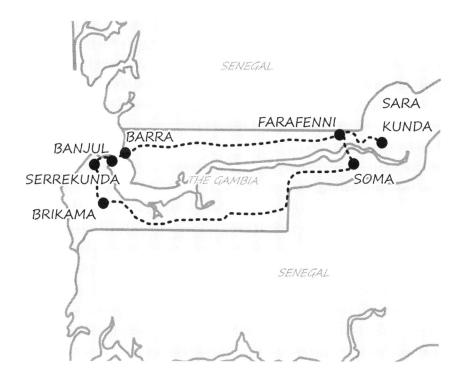

THIRTY

The Gambia is different

Moments after stepping off the plane in Banjul, olive-clad Gambian officials pulled Sutay and me out of line and into a back room. They were denying us our visitor seals because, they said, there was no room in our passports for their stamps.

The Gambia is a skinny, snakelike country, roughly 20 miles wide and piercing the larger nation of Senegal, which surrounds it on three sides. The country follows the curves of the Gambia River, spanned by not a single bridge, and there are only two main roads, the North Bank Road and the South Bank Road, each following the river and accessing a handful of vital ferry crossings.

About twice the size of Delaware, The Gambia is the smallest country in continental Africa, but it played an enormous role in my wife's biography. Sutay was born and raised in Colorado, but The Gambia is the place that gave her the name she uses today. It is the place where she attended her first childbirth, the place where the direction of her life changed course and the seeds of her career as a registered nurse and doula working with labor and delivery took hold.

This was her first time back. Returning to a place is a different animal than seeing it for the first time, especially to a country where one knows the language, dress, and customs, and where one has such strong memories.

By the time we'd reached The Gambia, Sutay and I had been on the road for most of the two years we'd known each other. So many cramped guesthouses, bush taxis, train berths, sickbeds, and other forced intimacies had certainly brought us closer together, and I thought we knew each other pretty well. But I had never seen my wife on edge the way she was as we entered The Gambia.

The lead officer told Sutay to wait in the hall and watch the bags. He wanted to deal with me because I was the man, even though this was *her* turf! Waves of past indignities in this place streamed behind her eyes; she left the room fuming.

———

It was important that I see The Gambia and get a taste of what it must have been like for her, no matter how short (or difficult) our visit. Plus, if we were going to grow old together, we would need to be able to visually place each other's endless tales that would begin with either, "Once, in Nicaragua..." or, "One time, in Sara Kunda..."

We'd come to The Gambia with a plan to travel east on the South Bank Road, stay overnight at Tendaba Camp, continue to the Soma ferry, cross the river to the north bank, then take a final series of vehicles to Sara Kunda, Sutay's old Peace Corps site, where we would arrive, unannounced, eight years after she'd last been there.

That was the idea. But as my wife had told me more than once, things didn't always go according to plan in The Gambia.

"I've traveled a little bit, you know," I said.

"The Gambia is different," she said.

The officer played on his power trip and allowed us one provisional night in the country until we received the proper seal the following day at the central immigration office in Banjul. We spent the night in a dormitory for church groups across the street from the Peace Corps office, where, the next morning, we asked the director for a letter inviting us into the country as "trainers." To make it legit, we offered to lead a session with the current group of trainees at Tendaba Camp, where we needed to go anyway.

Letter in hand, we took a cab downtown, passing beneath Arch 22, the ornate, white $1 million arch that President Yahya Jammeh built in 1996 to celebrate his military coup d'état of two years earlier. That was the year Sutay first arrived in The Gambia, just after the coup, when Yahya was very popular. In those days, he contracted with foreign companies to complete road projects and other public works; he erected thousands of billboards with his face on them; and he dedicated monuments to himself, like Arch 22, a structure so ridiculous, it contained the country's only elevator.

Ten years later, Yahya, who by the way, fully ordained himself "His Excellency Sheikh Professor Alhaji Dr. Yahya Abdul-Azziz Jemus Junkung Jammeh," was still in power (twice "reelected"), the billboards and monuments were well kept, but as we would soon find out, the roads were crumbling.

The immigration office was housed in an old building in central Banjul that smelled of mold and urine. Junked computers and other debris were piled under the stairs and in corners. We entered a second-story office and sat down before four brown-uniformed officers who sat side by side, elbow to elbow, behind a row of battered desks.

They discussed our case and perused our passports, handing them back and forth. After over a year of traveling, it was true that space was scarce in our worn, weathered blue booklets, which were curved from sweaty pockets and pouches. But come on, guys—just give us the stamps.

The first man thumbed through the ink-covered pages, roughly, backward and forward, forward and backward, as if blank sheets would sprout from his persistence. When none did, he passed the book to the next man who repeated the process. A sign on the wall behind the frowning officials said, "Happy Moments, Praise Allah; Difficult Moments, Seek Allah; Painful Moments, Trust Allah; Every Moment, Thank Allah."

I tried to find some peace in that, but as their inaction bore down, as they continued to rifle the pages, I could stand it no longer and blurted out, "We can order more pages, just let us—"

A kick to my shin stopped my attempt at conversation, which Sutay told me afterward could have resulted in orders to go to the U.S. Embassy on the other side of the city to order more passport pages, turning one morning's hassle into an all-week affair. Finally, after we paid a suddenly announced "document fee," the men found room for their Gambian stamp atop our Ugandan visas.

We celebrated our success by snipping at each other over a rushed lunch of oily, ginger-soaked chicken *yassa*, followed by a 2-hour series of deceitful taxi drivers before arriving at Brikama car park at three in the afternoon. Even though we'd gotten the stamps, our nerves were worn thin; it was hot, the air was dirty, and our day's journey up-country was just beginning.

THIRTY-ONE

Last car
to Soma

Dust, flies, and plastic danced across the lot, scudding the orange, hard-packed earth between rows of brightly painted buses. The vehicles were decorated with crudely drawn eyes above headlights, hand-painted prayers, faded flags, torn stickers, and Nike swooshes. A few buses were about to leave, piled high with teetering loads of luggage and livestock—goats bleating, exhaust spewing, departure imminent. I hoped for one of these; two seats left, we jump in, and off we go!

"Soma moto ley?" asked Sutay. Where is the Soma car?

The drivers shook their heads and pointed farther into the lot. I watched their loaded vehicles drive away; then I looked up at the pounding, descending sun.

The Gambia's sole bus company had gone bankrupt years before, replaced by a loose, unorganized mob of independent Mercedes trucks with *"Bisumilah!"* ("In the name of God!") and other religious declarations painted across their hoods and windshields. The roads were so poor now, only so many vehicles existed in the country that were sturdy enough to make the trip.

In Thailand, we rode in *tuk-tuks*. In Ghana they were called *tro-tros*. In The Gambia, the main transports were *gilly-gillies*. They were all variations of the "bush taxi" or "chicken bus," and a small fleet of them was parked at Brikama. We just had to locate the right one.

"Don't get to Brikama after midday," we'd been warned at the Peace Corps office during our briefing on how to get to Tendaba Camp. We'd been held up by bureaucracy in the capital and arrived late, and now had little choice except to find a ride.

I followed my wife across the packed dirt, trying to keep up as she guided me through a surreal landscape of rotten fruit, vendors, biting ants, feces, beaten dogs, and diesel-stained puddles. In addition to our backpacks, we carried cheap, woven bags brimming with fabric, fruit, and other gifts. Hospitality is offered freely in The Gambia, but guests are required to bring *silafondo*. We would be especially responsible for bringing gifts since our hosts, two days up-country, did not know we were coming.

––––––––

"Asalaam aleikum," Sutay said, as we emerged from an alley of red, yellow, and green cars.

"Aleikum salaam," responded the man sitting there. He wore an ankle-length, purple *dendiko* and mirrored sunglasses. The man had a bare, bald head. He sprawled on a bench next to an empty vehicle. He and Sutay gently touched right hands in greeting, then brought their hands to their chests.

Watching Sutay don her African skin as we moved through the continent was a high point that I'll never forget. Long-unspoken words, grunts, expressions, and body language flowed from her mouth, hands, eyes, and poise. I'm not sure who was more surprised—Sutay as she rediscovered behavior from her past, The Gambians, who were not used to *toubab* foreigners knowing their language, or me, seeing this whole new part of my wife come alive.

Bright, tie-dyed cloth draped Sutay's shoulders and curves; a matching *tiko* squeezed her head, protecting her long hair from the dust. In The Gambia, Sutay's body remained tense the entire time we were there, which was unusual for her. Her neck stiffened and extended, a periscope peering up and around, watching out for the both of us. I loved this woman, so protective of me and proud!

"Kaira-be," she said. Peace be upon you.

"Kaira-dorong," the man responded. Peace only.

"Soma moto ley?" Sutay asked.

"It just left," the man said in English. "But I am going to Soma. You will go in my car."

A vast charcoal cloud slipped in front of the sun.

"My name is Mohammed," he said. We took a closer look at his vehicle. It was a big boxy über-van, covered with bright paint, stickers, and posters. One window sported a Rolling Stones tongue and the smiling, waving portrait of "Le Frère Muammar al-Kadhafi." Near the center of the windshield was a six-inch American flag, stripes faded into whiteness so that only the blue field behind the stars and the letters "U.S.A." remained. The flag was next to a black-and-white sticker bearing Osama bin Laden's face (I have pictures to prove it!). In the middle of the windshield, in the most prominent position, there was a poster of President Yahya taped to the glass. Even though it blocked half the driver's field of view, Yahya's waving presence would, I presumed, ease our way through checkpoints and trouble.

"It is the last car today," he said.

"Where are you from?" asked Mohammed.

"America," I said.

"America! Fine-fine! Where are you going?"

"Tendaba Camp," said Sutay.

"Fine-fine!" said Mohammed. "You are welcome!"

"We will leave soon?"

"Inshallah!"

Of course. The definition of *inshallah*, a common term in The Gambia, ranges from the literal "if God wills it" to, as Paul Theroux observed, the imminently more realistic translation, "not bloody likely."

Three passengers were standing next to Mohammed's car, talking idly and, in slow motion it seemed, fending off flies and hawkers. We joined them. We would leave when there were enough passengers.

The sun dipped lower. The sky grew grayer. We claimed seats, then waited outside the *gilly-gilly* as vendors of random goods approached us, mostly barefoot children, wide eyes shaded by baskets of wares on their heads. None passed the opportunity to stand and stare at the pink, sweating foreigners. The children looked at us mostly in silence. They couldn't tell if we were potential clients or animals in a zoo, so instead of offering us their fruit, cigarettes, plastic toys, and roasted corn, they just stared.

Mohammed called to a boy selling stickers from a battered cardboard box. I watched through waves of heat as he pored over images of famous *imams*, stopping to give me a short lesson about each bearded face: "This man is from Senegal. He is a very holy man. He is 93 years old and he has eighty wives!"

There were also Western cartoon characters and country flags from all over, but Mohammed stopped at an oversized laminate of Madonna, not the holy mother, but the singer, circa her kiss-blowing "Like a Virgin" days. He used a rag to wipe the dust from his car's back window and stuck her on. Her sultry, lip-glossed face joined bin Laden, Gaddafi, and Jagger. Mohammed looked to us for approval and we shot him a couple of thumbs-up.

The afternoon wore on and the sky continued to darken with clouds. A faint smell of rain appeared. We would be traveling at night, an eventuality I tried to avoid on the already-dangerous roads in countries like this. But we had nowhere to stay in Brikama, couldn't return to Banjul, and less than a week to make it up-country to Sara Kunda, deliver our gifts, and return for our flight to Casablanca—and home.

Mohammed didn't care about our tight schedule. Finally, a group of eight chatty women showed up who appeared to know him, and he finally gave the order to load up. Even though Sutay and I had staked out seats hours before, it was a mad melee. I pushed through elbows, knees, and luggage, forcing myself into the tiny space between my wife and a burly matron with two children in her arms. The roof rocked with the luggage being transferred to it, and the crying of goats was followed by a trickle of urine outside our windowless window.

Mohammed climbed into the driver's seat. It was time to go. We were off, and started lumbering out of the parking lot and out of town. But first he had to buy gifts.

"When we arrive in Soma," he explained, turning around to talk to us, "the first thing they will say is, 'Where are our mangos?'"

"'Silafondo-ley?'" Sutay said, giving just the right rise to the last syllable. It was Mandinka for "Where's my gift?" She was using the phrase Mohammed's family would use when they greeted him that night, and he laughed at her accuracy.

"You know! How do you know *silafondo-ley?*" he asked.

Sutay told him the story of how she had lived for two and a half years in a village called Sara Kunda.

"Near Farefenni, on the north bank?"

Sutay nodded. "Tomorrow we'll take the ferry at Soma," she said.

At a roadside stand, the multitude of brightly clad women piled out of our car and haggled while Mohammed smoked a cigarette next to our window and explained that these were his brothers' wives and children. "I am bringing them home to Soma," he said.

The women shouted and clamored with the mango sellers until each had come to some agreement and the fruit was gathered into bags and baskets. They piled back in the car—swaddled infants, bags of mangos, quiet toddlers—and we departed Brikama at exactly the hour I'd hoped to be arriving in Tendaba, still a five-hour drive away. At least we were moving.

"No to coup! Yes to democracy!" read a hand-scrawled sign on the side of the road. President Yahya smiled and waved from our windshield. We asked Mohammed if the government was planning to fix the road.

"The North Bank Road they are fixing," he said. "The Taiwanese, they are fixing it. But the government wants the same company for the South Bank Road, so we are waiting."

"How long have you been waiting?"

"Eight years."

"What has changed in that time?" I asked.

"Yahya is fatter," he said, grinning.

THIRTY-TWO

Sara Kunda homecoming

Sara Kunda is a north bank village, located not quite halfway up the Gambia River. Sutay had been taken in by an extended family there for two years. During her Peace Corps service there, Farefenni, a crossroads town on the north bank was the closest place where she could get a cold drink (or at least a warm beer), news from the outside world (or at least from the Peace Corps office in Banjul), fax a letter to her mother, and maybe converse in English with a fellow *toubab* if any international volunteers also happened to be in town.

We arrived in Farefenni via a precarious river ferry in a long, canoe-like boat. In the market, we fended off flies as we picked up a few last gifts and supplies, then walked to the corner where the leaning, broken *moto* to Sara Kunda was parked.

For me, an Africa travel rookie, everything in The Gambia was new—every moment a raw, exciting discovery. For Sutay, it was complicated. Ten years before, when she moved into her mud-and-stick hut in the Sabally family compound, she was dubbed "Sutay Sabally," the adopted daughter and personal guest of Sarjo Njara Sabally, whom she called "Baba." Baba gave her the name in a traditional Mandinka naming ceremony, or *kulio*. It had actually been a double *kulio*, to name both the foreign volunteer and the baby who had been born the day she arrived. Everyone in the compound dressed in his or her finest, brightest outfits. Food was prepared, music arranged.

Baba whispered to her, "Sutay Sabally." And so she was. The name means "recognize." Sutay was the only foreigner to ever have lived in Sara Kunda—she was easy to recognize. Baba then shaved a piece of hair from the baby's head and cut a piece off of Sutay's braid. He and other elders made pronouncements and read from the Koran. Baba poured a few drops of water on the girls' foreheads and asked the village oral history keepers if they'd heard what these two new children would be called. They answered, "Yes, and our lips are sealed."

As we climbed onto the last vehicle, I watched Sutay retreat further behind her *tiko* and shades, her thoughts spiraling as we drew even closer to Sara Kunda. So much had changed in her life since she'd left. But what had changed in Sara Kunda? Had it been modernized? Had it gotten worse? Baba could be gone, she feared, the family moved; her dog, Danjung, surely hadn't survived... They had no idea we were coming, and

Sutay had had no way to communicate with them. If nobody recognized her, where would we sleep?

———————

Two months after her *kulio*, Sutay's initiation to the village continued when, on one clear, warm night, Baba's daughter, Fatou, went into labor in the hut next to hers. Sutay was still a new, doe-eyed volunteer who barely understood the language. But she understood that Fatou's mother, Nkombe, the village midwife, wanted to play the role of mother for this birth. Sutay, the knowledgeable *toubab*, would be the midwife, they decided. They didn't know, nor did they care, that Sutay had zero training or experience in delivering babies—nor that her participation in a birth totally violated Peace Corps policy.

Sutay's first instinct was to take Fatou to Ngen, the nearest village where there was a clinic with electricity and a nurse. Baba summoned a donkey cart, and the three women—Fatou, Nkombe, and Sutay—climbed aboard to ride eight miles or so, in the light of a full moon, to cricket chirps and hyena howls, bouncing over the rutted path as Fatou's contractions grew closer.

When they arrived, finding neither electricity nor nurse, they entered the dark clinic and Sutay positioned Fatou on the concrete birthing slab on her back, as she'd seen on television, her only reference. She lit two candles to place between Fatou's knees, and after some pushing, out came the baby—both Fatou's and Sutay's first. Sutay continued with her TV nursing; she held the baby upside down and spanked her bottom before tying and cutting the cord with a razor from her med kit, then placing the baby on her mother's chest. After a while, they rode back to Sara Kunda with the magic of new life bundled between them as the sun came up.

───────────

At her old Sara Kunda bus stop she recognized so well, we got down, shouldered our bags, and walked from the traveling tree on the edge of the village. Children saw us and arrived first, helping with our bags even though they had no idea who we were; our group grew as we rounded each corner. Both our hearts quickened as we got nearer the compound. Finally, with about twenty or thirty people in tow, Sutay and I marched unannounced and unexpected into the Sabally compound.

"Sutay! Sutay!"

They hopped up and down and hugged her as chaos reigned and more people appeared.

"Sutay Sabally!"

The shouts were as much exclamations of disbelief as they were of affection. At home, in the United States, her name was anything but convenient, drawing puzzled stares, uncomfortable silences, and mispronunciations. But here in Sara Kunda, "Sutay" was *who she was*. And seeing her in a place where people knew her name, how to pronounce it, what it meant, where it came from, was like watching a mysterious piece of my partner click into place.

"Sutay! Sutay!"

She responded with rapid Mandinka greetings, surprising herself as forgotten responses bubbled up from her past while dozens of women grasped her and held her and continued crying her name.

I stood to the side, filming and snapping until Sutay yanked me into the knot of people and introduced me by interlocking her index fingers together, declaring our matrimony. New cheers erupted along with claps on my back and smiles! Tears streaming from behind Sutay's sunglasses and from the eyes of those clutching her mixed with the dirt at our feet.

Someone led her to Danjung. Her old, white *wuolo* dog was living the royal life on Baba's porch. In a society that mistreats animals as a national pastime, people were boasting to Sutay that they had fed her dog while she was gone and allowed him to sleep on their porch. Seeing Danjung always made them think of her, they said (because he'd belonged to her, but also because he was white).

Baba appeared and the crowd parted. He greeted Sutay formally as he held her hand and the family watched. Baba was a serious, 68-year-old Mandinka man of few words and innumerable folds carved into his masklike face.

"Asalaam aleikum," she said.

"Aleikum salaam," said Baba. They both touched their own chests.

"Kaira-be," she said. Peace be upon you.

"Kaira-dorong," said Baba. Peace only.

"Kori tenante?" asked Sutay.

"Tenante." I am fine, he said.

"Sumolu ley?" asked Sutay. Where is the family?

"Abije," said Baba. They are there.

"And your wife?"

"Abije." She is there.

"Grandmother?"

"Abije."

"Your siblings?"

"Abije."

The exchange continued and then was repeated as they reversed roles, so that Baba now asked Sutay, "Sumolu ley?" and she told him everyone was back home in America. They were there and they were fine.

With a click of his tongue, Baba ended the greeting and said, "Famo-kettah!" Long time!

Sutay answered with her own exclamatory click. "B'lai." It's true.

Baba had watched over Sutay, ensuring her shelter, food, protection, and honor. He had saved her life once, arranging transport to the clinic in Farefenni after Konko, Sutay's adopted brother, had found her deathly ill, sprawled unconscious behind her hut, in vomit and diarrhea and raging with fever.

Baba turned to me and spoke in Mandinka with Sutay translating, "Sutay Sabally is my daughter. Now you are her husband, so I give you the name 'Lamin Sabally.'"

Baba never stopped looking me in the eyes as he took my hands in his and pressed them. *Lamin* was the name given to all firstborn Mandinka sons. And so it was.

THIRTY-THREE

Toma

Just as the thrill of our arrival was calming down, Fatou pushed a child forward, a 10-year-old, almond-eyed beauty with a red *tiko* tied on her head and a shy curve to her body. In The Gambia, if someone shares your name, they are your toma, and this is how you refer to each other. Ten years before, on a hyena-howling night in the candle-lit clinic in Ngen, Fatou had named her daughter Sutay, to honor her new friend and *toubab* sister who had helped her.

After a moment of silence, my wife and the little girl shouted "*Toma!*" and embraced.

We moved our things into Konko's hut. Konko had been Sutay's scrawny 12-year-old sidekick when she lived here. He was now a muscular, 22-year-old bachelor with his own peanut field and decent English. When Sutay's Mandinka failed her,

Konko stayed by our side to serve as translator and guide. He saw it as a chance to both visit with his sister and improve his future.

"Sutay!" he said smiling. "Take me to America! Find me an American wife!" He was helping us move into his room, and trying to hang our mosquito net over his rough straw mattress.

"Konko," she said, "you can't be lazy in America. The women there won't allow it. You have to cook and clean and work."

"I don't care!" he said. "Take me, I'll cook, I'll clean!"

***

The next afternoon, Konko invited us to drink *attaya*, a cheap, powdered Chinese black tea whose elaborate, time-consuming, three-cup brewing and drinking etiquette was the basis for most conversations and social gatherings in the country. Sutay preferred to stay on the women's *bantaba*, a raised platform where they sat together and talked for hours; she barely noticed as I disappeared into the bachelors' hut.

Most of our time in Sara Kunda we spent sitting, drinking tea, and communicating however we could. While Sutay floated throughout the compound on waves of nostalgia, I doggie-paddled in various streams of stimuli.

The young men of Sutay's compound, her brothers (my brothers now), wanted to show me some rural Gambian hospitality. They began the tea ceremony with the first round, giving me syrupy sweet shots of *attaya* after it was poured from great heights into tiny shot glasses. Only after we finished did they tell me it was special *attaya*, brewed with *yahmo*, or *ganja*. The unexpected warm buzz crept into my body, led to a slow-motion round of the giggles (universal language), and compounded with the heat until I drifted off to our room and into our mosquito net womb for a few hours of dreams. When I awoke, the sun was down and the stars were out.

I approached my brethren outside on the men's *bantaba*. They were all still there.

"Come, Lamin!" they shouted. "We are starting the third round of tea! Don't worry! This *attaya* is not special like before!"

————————

The next morning, Fatou fell ill with a malaria attack. That's how the disease works, by launching surges of sickness from your liver, knocking you down, letting you back up, knocking you down again. Fatou's daughter, 10-year-old Sutay, took up the multiple burdens of caring for her bedridden mother, her baby brother, and us, her mother's guests. After starting a fire and pounding grain, this little girl ran to the market to buy tins of fish and bouillon cubes; she carried a huge bucket of water on her head; ground onions and tomatoes with a giant pestle; cooked our meal over a stick fire; then, as we ate, cooled her mother with a wicker fan.

When my wife took over the fan and placed Fatou's head, screaming with fever, in her own lap, little Sutay, relieved of her duties, sprang up to sing and play with her friends, their brightly wrapped cloths around skinny hips and shirtless skinny torsos, their heads topped in cotton *tikos*. The girls played pat-a-cake games and they laughed as I took their video.

THIRTY-FOUR

Baba's blessing

"Allaaaaaaaaaaah hu-akbar!"

The old speakers of the mosque made the song soft and strained. The sky was dark and star-sprinkled, just as it had been when we'd gone to sleep only a few hours before, and it was already the first call to prayer. The boys hadn't eaten the last of the goat—hunks of meat served with baguettes and fried onions—until after midnight. The party had broken up soon after the feast was finished.

Sutay and I were barely awake, awash in candlelight and beginning to bathe when the *imam* called again.

"*Allaaaaaaaaaaah hu-akbar!*"

This refrain that had sounded five times a day for more than half a millennium in this far-off fold of West Africa was but one layer of the waking village soundscape—crickets, roosters, goats, songbirds, and other creatures joined in the declaration of God's greatness.

Sutay and I took turns squatting next to the plastic bucket of well water to bathe. Stars were fading as we prepared for a long day of travel back to Banjul.

The well water, which Sutay had collected the previous day and carried here on her head in a plastic container, to the supportive hoots of the village women, was earthy and cool, and the night's perspiration rinsed from my neck and splashed down my back. I closed my eyes to the sensation and tried to wrap my mind around all that had happened the previous night, and everything we'd experienced during our week in The Gambia.

Rain-smells, mud, soaked greens, oily browns, picking thin bones of fish from salty bowls of groundnut stew—this was The Gambia I would remember. Sweet *attaya* tea, the hot, funky crush inside dilapidated deathtrap *gilly-gillies*, sketchy boat rides across the wide river . . . through it all, Sutay and I had moved together, and were still moving.

The sky continued to lighten, but the sun was still not up. Bathed, dressed, and packed, we emerged from the house and walked to Baba's, the largest hut, in the center of the compound, where we found him sitting with Miriama, his newest wife.

"Isama!" Sutay said, entering the house. Good morning.

"Isama!" said everyone.

"Kaira-be?" Do you have peace?

"Kaira-dorong." Peace only.

"Sumolu ley?" How is your family?

"Abije. Abije." They are there. They are fine.

The greetings continued. Even at this early hour, at the solemn occasion of our farewell, there was still time to recite the list of greetings. When they were finished, Sutay and I sat down on short, worn, wooden stools and talked with Baba and Miriama about how delicious the goat meat had tasted. Baba had not come to our party. After slitting the goat's neck while Konko and three brothers held down the writhing body, his role was finished, and he'd listened to the festivities from his quarters. There had been drumming—the women had played on plastic buckets with their hands and sang, "Sutay ben-doli-do-lah, Lamin ben-doli-do-lah!" Because Sutay is here we are dancing, we are dancing because Sutay and Lamin are here!

I'd contributed a verse about Sutay's dog: "Danjung ben-doli-do-lah!" causing hysterical laughter.

"Everyone very happy!" said Baba.

"When we have our own *din-dingos*," Sutay said about our future children, "we will bring them to Sara Kunda."

"I will perform a *kulio* for them," promised Baba.

"Inshallah!" I said. God willing.

"Inshallah!" he said.

Just then, the sun blasted into the day and into the room, splattering the back wall with color. Miriama stood up and pointed to Sutay, pronouncing her name one last time, "Sutay Sabally," then firmly squeezed her own breast.

Konko translated, "She said, 'I am Sutay's mother.'"

Miriama then pointed to me. "Lamin Sabally," she said, then squeezed her breast. She pointed to both of us while sweeping her other arm toward Baba. "Beh keelin," she said.

"We are all one," translated Sutay.

Baba's eyes hardened and the creases in his face were pronounced by the sideways light. He gestured that we approach him and Miriama. We were standing close, the four of us. Baba took my hands in his, opened them upward, leaned forward, and whispered a quiet stream of Arabic ending with a puff of air blown into my palms. He did the same for Sutay. My hands felt weightless as they drifted down to my sides.

We stepped outside, Baba, Miriama, Konko, and me. Danjung joined us outside, his old stump of a tail pumping back and forth. Fatou and little Sutay arrived as we walked in silence through the compound entrance. Seeing her Toma cry, little Sutay also burst into tears but was confused about why everyone was so sad. Before we reached the edge of the village, Baba and the others took their leave. There were more tears and pressed hands, then dirt-crunching footsteps as we parted.

Sutay and I walked to the traveling tree and placed our bags on the ground. There was a Wolof border guard there wearing a brown uniform, on his way to work. There was a Fula woman with a recently cheek-scarred infant tied to her back. There was a wizened *marabout* leaning against his staff. And there were Sutay and me. We all stood in the center of the crossroads and waited for a vehicle to appear.

THIRTY-FIVE

North Bank Road

The extended sunrise in Sara Kunda that morning was serene and full of sorrow. Maybe one day we would return, marching into the village unannounced as we'd just done to visit Sutay's adopted Gambian family. Maybe not.

Even after Baba and the family had left us by the tree and the tears had stopped, everything remained heavy and frustrating. A silent, bouncy ride took us to Farefenni, where we learned that President Yahya had declared a "national cleanup day," resulting in an unexpected six-hour layover at the bus station. No transport was allowed to operate while everyone was busy picking up trash. Which they weren't. Everyone just sat around watching the trash blow in the wind, waiting for the government decree to lift.

We plopped atop our bags and I messed with my camera. A man shouted me down for taking photographs—the first time on our entire trip this had happened. I put it away and backed off. When it was time to go, we had to physically fight for our seats, and jealous shouts and elbows jabbed us as we piled in and got under way.

The road was so pitted, pocked, and potholed that we proceeded mostly on the shoulder even when it pitched the vehicle at an absurd angle. When the shoulder grew steep or rutted, the driver would diagonal his way to the other side. I wondered how many extra miles this zig-zagging added to the trip.

Three hours later, the *gilly-gilly* broke down and the men got out to push. I heaved with the others, ankle-deep in mud and looking at the dark sky ahead. Somewhere to the left, beyond the verdant rice fields, was the Gambia River, a powerful presence even when not in sight; we'd crossed it once, a wide, muddy muscle that twisted the length of the country. If we made it to Barra, we would cross it once again that evening, completing our multi-transport loop back to Banjul.

By the time we were traveling again, the sun had disappeared and the dark patch of sky we'd spied earlier had become an opaque curtain getting closer and closer. The air was orange with light and electricity; thunder pulsed from the clouds to our bellies and we lurched toward the wall of rain. Through the clot of people in the vehicle, I saw the driver tense his arms on the big wheel.

And then we were in it.

The windows were a mangled blur. The roof was hammered with sheets of water. Visibility hit zero when a swath of red mud splattered the windshield, eclipsing everything. The vehicle leaned into the ditch. We were engulfed in water, noise, and darkness.

I grabbed Sutay and held her close as we leaned even more. One of the women screamed for Allah, her ululations silenced by a crack of lightning. In the instant I felt the bus tipping. For a split second, or who-knows-how-long, I thought we were done for, that this was how our trip, our marriage, and our lives would end. I braced myself in that instant of weightlessness. Then we swerved, the vehicle righted, and the rain was behind us.

Just like that.

The sun was low, wet, and powerful now, blasting through the windshield and making everything glow—from the torn strands of seat cushion stuffing to the garish patterns on the women's *tikos* and *dendikos*. The side of Sutay's face was alight as she looked out the window and then at me, tears like jewels on her cheek. We'd made it.

———————

We'd made it through the storm. We'd made it to Sara Kunda, where we'd delivered gifts to Baba and I'd learned about the Africa chapter of my wife's life. Her time in The Gambia had not only made her who she is, but had pointed her straight toward me like a bow shooting an arrow.

We'd made it through these new experiences together that would last a lifetime—like this epic sunset, which was going on and on and on as we drove through it. The sky was beyond belief; a colossal canvas, a vast ceiling of clouds lit from below with salmons, reds, pinks, and purples. Air blew in through the windows and it was wet and fresh, the first tolerable temperature we'd felt all week. It washed away the waiting, the fighting among passengers, the struggles, and we were all just there, riding together. Behind a baobab tree, a rainbow appeared, arcing from the canopy and disappearing into post-storm mist.

A heavy-flying heron skimmed the rice tops and rose on the wind.

The vehicle continued forward but time was as still as I had ever felt it, the colors lingering, heron gliding. As the last of the light tried to overtake us, the moment and the country stretched in every direction. The sky reflected in a thousand rain-filled potholes, silver mirrors that broke beneath our tires.

We'd made it.

It had not been easy nor had it always been comfortable. It was as if for every epiphany-laced, rainbow-colored travelgasm that The Gambia had to deliver, it had exacted a toll. From our tussle with immigration upon arrival to our up-country journey into my wife's past to a thousand interactions, memories, frustrations, and rewards in between . . . this skinny little country had bottlenecked all the intensity there was left in our trip, wringing it out in bursts of rain, sweat, and tears. I'd never had such an experience in my travels and never will again.

It—and we—kept going: driving into the night, then sprinting and panting to catch the last Barra–Banjul ferry, finding a taxi to Serrekunda, losing a bag in a shared bus, getting lost outside our guest house, saved in a dark back alley by a Good Samaritan....

So the next morning, I was surprised when Sutay said there was one more place she wanted to visit. I just wanted to curl up in bed and wait till it was time to go to the airport.

"I want to go to Kachikally," she said, her hands instinctively rising to her belly. "I want to see the crocodiles."

THIRTY-SIX

Crocodile love

"This is important," Sutay said, in a tone that made me believe her. "It's is not a zoo. It's different—and it's close, don't worry."

But I did. The Gambia was a small, intense country that had been one of the most difficult to navigate on our trip. The previous day, to return to Banjul, we'd gotten stuck, nearly crashed in a storm, almost missed the ferry, and lost a camera. Now we were safe and sound in the capital, one simple taxi ride from the airport—and our flight to Casablanca. I didn't understand Sutay's urge to head to a swampy corner of the city to see a bunch of crocodiles, but I stopped saying anything and just got into the cab with her.

The taxi driver drove us past the tourist beaches of Bakau (where Gambian male prostitutes called "bumsters" prowled the hotels for foreign sugar mamas and clients) and dropped us at the end of a short lane in Old Town. From there, Sutay, by some thread of memory, guided us through a confusing maze of pitted neighborhood streets. We stepped over sewage ditches as we looked for nonexistent signs to the pond.

"I didn't really get it either," she said to me as we walked, "the first time I heard about them. But I went anyway. It was at the end of my Peace Corps service here. Some friends and I came to Kachikally and asked for a blessing, which is what our Gambian friends told us to do."

"Did yours come true?" I asked.

She just smiled as we entered the small visitor center. A guide there explained that the same family, the Bojang clan, had tended the pond and animals at Kachikally for hundreds of years and still does today. We read on the displays that the crocodiles were tame and that many people believed the water has supernatural powers. Childless women traveled from around the region to Kachikally to ask for babies, and men came to ask for power—or help winning a wrestling match or election.

The most famous of these was President Yahya Jammeh, who bathed with the crocodiles before the 1994 military coup that placed him in the president's palace where he still resides. One of his first actions as president was to put crocodiles on the Gambian currency. (One of his next, allege some, was to feed his political rivals to the same crocodiles.)

There were a few tribal items on display, mostly masks and musical instruments. But the real attraction, the reason we were there—more than a hundred Nile crocodiles living in and around a pond—was just through the other side of the building.

We stepped onto a muddy trail, enclosed in a tunnel of branches and leaves that twisted toward the pond. At the end, several hand-painted signs said not to touch any crocodile without the advice of the pool guide. On cue, a teenage guide appeared by our side. He asked us to sign a visitor's book and told us not to touch the crocodiles' heads or mouths.

"Everything else, okay!" he said.

A bright green blanket of algae covered the surface of the water and the animals floating there, so that they looked molded to the water. Along the banks and paths and edges, crocs of all sizes lazed and waddled. A breeze had scattered purple and yellow flower petals about the place, many of which stuck to the animals' heads and skins.

It was raining, a slight, warm drizzle, and we crept down the slope, stepping around flat, heavy animals, and crouching near a group of them at the water's edge. Sutay removed a cloth bag from her shoulder. She squatted in the middle of three or four medium-sized crocodiles. They remained motionless.

I tried not to imagine the body-twisting, blood-spewing, water-spraying thrash-fest this could become. Instead, there were only the singing of cicadas, water dripping, and the laughter of the guards up the bank. Sutay methodically emptied her cache of icons, prayer beads, and other treasures she'd gathered during the past sixteen months onto the ground. She dipped each into the water, then touched it on the nearest crocodile's back.

I supported her by staying quiet as she completed her task. This was not the first fertility shrine we had visited. But it was the end of our trip, so it would be our last. Our plan was to start a family when we got home, so why not use all the help we could get? The crocodile next to Sutay's foot yawned in slow motion and we placed our hands on its warm, living back.

Eight months earlier in Darjeeling, India, Sutay and I had met a man named Rajah Banarjee, a living legend in the organic tea world. Banarjee is the larger-than-life owner of Makaibari Tea Estates, a model of progressive farming techniques. When I walked into his office, he was wearing his customary tan colonial bush outfit and his desk was covered with papers, photographs, and shrines to Ganesha, the elephant-headed, multi-armed Hindu deity. Behind Banarjee on the wall was an enormous blue "Om" symbol.

We were visiting his plantation to learn more about biodynamic farming practices on his tea garden, but before touring the grounds, we had spent several hours in his office, tasting tea and talking about religion, life, and children. Banarjee had a new grandchild, a large framed photo of whom was on his desk. I congratulated him. "No! These babies are not ours!" he shouted. "We are merely conduits!"

He had asked us if we planned on having children.

"Yes," we had said.

"But your children will not be yours! The souls of babies choose when and by whom they will each enter into this world," he had said.

These are the kinds of nuggets that I collected during our travels. While my wife was busy purchasing prayer beads in Bodh

Gaya or browsing statues of pregnant women in Ghanaian markets, I was scribbling my observations into a stack of precious pocket journals. A few of these bits of wisdom stuck with me, especially heavy pronouncements like Banarjee's.

Ernest Becker had a similar idea: "We don't know where babies come from.... 'Sperm and the egg!' Idiot answer. It's not an answer at all, it's merely a description of a speck in a causal process that is a mystery... You get married, you're sitting at a table having breakfast—there are two of you—and a year later there's somebody else sitting there.... They just came, literally, out of nowhere, and they keep growing in your environment. If you stop to think about it, which you don't, because it's annoying, it's upsetting, then it's a total mystery."

I looked at my wife across the crocodile's back and she looked at me and I loved her. If we were to be conduits for distant souls, players in "a total mystery," then bring it. We would be ready to be their parents, whether we understood what that meant or not. In the meantime, I loved Sutay and I loved that she had taken me to this strange, solemn place, crouching over a crocodile in the rain at Katchikally. I loved that the animal remained completely still, mouth gaping, eyes staring ahead. If it knew we were there, it ignored us, as did the entire bask of crocodiles in every direction, as if we were invisible. It was a warm, wet, wondrous moment.

I thought of the countless other experiences streaming behind us—riding up and down The Gambia, walking the streets of Accra, Rawalpindi, Mussoorie... Sure, I would have continued to travel had I never met this woman, but not like this.

Ours is a love, from the first to the last day of our trip, built on the pursuit of unpredictable, impossible moments, upon

which we feasted. Side by side, licking our chops for more. As
we finished our little silent ceremony, collected our things, and
got up to walk around, it kept drizzling and misting and then
it stopped, and then it rained again. After a while, we walked
back up the vine-draped trail, back through the visitor's center,
back onto the old streets of Bakau.

The rain was coming down harder now. We went back
to the guesthouse, dried off, collected our bags, and make a
beeline for Banjul International Airport. Of course, we had
plenty of time before our flight after all, proving our side trip
to Bakau was as important and worth the risk as Sutay had
promised it would be.

We breathed freely when we finally settled into our seats
on the flight to Senegal and then Morocco. Sutay looked out
the window, lost in stacks of place-based memories, while I
scratched and sketched on the final pages of my journal.

EPILOGUE

I'm loading our three beautiful daughters into the new mini-van. I lean in, buckle, snap, and secure. Shanti, 7, Zenlana, 5, and Sky, 2, relax into their car-seats, ready for anything. They have never been on a road trip this long and we have no idea how they will handle it. We'll find out soon enough.

Roof-box locked; sippy cups and coffee mugs in place; doors closed; ignition on; Mary Poppins soundtrack full blast; wheels up! Our first month-long, family car-camping adventure has begun. We will drive nearly 3000 miles around the state of Colorado, to national parks, national forests, playgrounds, and as many hot springs as we can work in to our big loop.

Sutay settles in next to me, posture straight, cheeks smooth and flushed, dark sunglasses pulled down, and a burgundy African *tiko* wrapped around her hair.

"How far is it to the spring-hots?" asks Zenlana.

My wife's mask of a face breaks into a soft, sudden smile as I answer, "It's about six hours to the first one."

"Is that a long time or a short time?" she asks.

"I'm not sure," I say. "Is Sky asleep yet?"

"No, she's holding my finger."

Our family is formed and complete. I married one woman and now I have four to take care of, but I don't stop to think about it. There isn't time. I have two jobs, three children, and as many bills and hassles as we foresaw. I glance at Sutay next to me.

Sometimes, everything speeds along like a torrent of change, months and years zinging by, our children changing daily. Other times, time stands still in heart-stopping moments of fear and clarity, like when I first let go of Shanti's bicycle seat and she pedaled down the driveway without me. Or that moment during our honeymoon, when Sutay and I were walking the grounds of Wat Pho and we stumbled upon a giant golden penis six feet tall.

It was a thing to admire, larger than life, complete with gleaming foreskin and veins, pointed straight up at the white monsoon sky. The temple brochure said the icon represented the phallus of Shiva the Destroyer himself, ruler of the Hindu pantheon whose fiery "lingam of light" had once beamed across the universe to begin time. To honor Shiva, I read, "followers offer milk and bilwa leaves to the phallus . . . women who pray to become fertile for pregnancy will return here if their wish is fulfilled, to place another phallus at the shrine in thanks."

Sure enough, we watched as one Thai couple knelt, palms pressed to their chests and holding long sticks of incense. White, clovey smoke rose into the sky. After they walked away, a young Indian woman in a sari approached, bowed her head, and prayed silently; then another couple stepped up and posed for a photo. Everyone did something slightly different, unique, but presumably, all wanting the same thing: a baby.

We'd come to Wat Pho that day to see the 150-foot-long Parinirvana Buddha, reclining across a great hall with mother-of-pearl eyes and 108 sacred etchings on 15-foot-high feet, at the moment of his death. We felt small as we circled it with hundreds of other visitors, everyone whispering and taking pictures. Outside, in the gardens, Sutay and I joined monks, tourists, and temple cats on stone paths lined with stupas, chedis, more Buddhas—which led us to the gleaming specimen before us.

At first, we sat to the side and watched as people approached and touched the statue. Then it was our turn. Or was it?

How do you know when you're ready to have children? Living out of backpacks and cheap guesthouses, we certainly were not. Not at that moment. Yet why else were we taking this trip? Why else had such objects appeared in our path again and again?

Standing before Shiva's glory, pondering our unborn children—it was like a tentacle from the future reaching back to give us a gentle nudge. Without looking at each other, we stood up, stepped toward the icon, and touched the warm metal, our hands overlapping.

Ten years later, we are as deep in the squeeze of parental existence as we can be. One of the things that has kept me going through these exhausting years is the knowledge that one day, we will be through these early, sleep-deprived stages, or at least to a point where the baby isn't so fragile and our oldest can help care for her little sisters. When that happens, I thought for years, our family will set out for new horizons and have so many adventures together. One day.

It crept up quickly.

The road glimmers with heat through the wide windshield. I turn on to the highway and sing along with my girls who are practically shouting with the music: "Let's go fly a kite, up to the highest height!"

We pick up speed as we leave the city behind and soar into the mountains.

THE END

BIBLIOGRAPHY

Becker, Ernest, "Growing up rugged," a talk given at the University of British Columbia, Vancouver, Canada, on November 13, 1970; first published in *The Gestalt Journal, Volume XVI, Number 2* (Fall, 1993).

Bennett, Arnold, The Honeymoon: A Comedy in Three Acts, originally published 1910.

Forster, E.M., *A Passage to India* (Harcourt Brace, 1924).

Kamenetz, Rodger, *The Jew in the Lotus: A Poet's Rediscovery of Jewish Identity in Buddhist India* (Harper, 1994).

Lapierre, Dominique, *City of Joy* (Grand Central Publishing, 1985).

Naipaul, V.S., *India: A Wounded Civilization* (Vintage, 2003).

Pelton, Robert Young, *The World's Most Dangerous Places* (Harper, 1994).

Potts, Rolf, *Vagabonding: An Uncommon Guide to the Art of Long-Term World Travel* (Villard Books, 2002).

Stewart, Ralph Randles, *Flora of Pakistan: History and Exploration of Plants in Pakistan and Adjoining Areas* (1982).

Theroux, Paul. *Dark Star Safari: Overland from Cairo to Capetown* (Mariner Books, 2004).

RECIPE: DEBASISH'S KICHURI

Yields enough for four people

1 cup uncooked white rice
1 cup lentils
Fresh ginger, as much as you want, mashed with pestle
2 onions, chopped
Garlic (don't be shy), minced
Green hot chilies to taste, sliced lengthwise
Pinches of salt and sugar
2 cups cut carrots, string beans, eggplant, etc.

1. Place all contents except the cut vegetables in a medium-size pot and mix thoroughly.

2. Add the veggies and mix further; adjust spices to taste.

3. Add 5 cups filtered water to pot and cover, or place "hodge-podge" and water in rice cooker.

4. Cook until all the water is absorbed.

5. Eat.

6. Belch out loud. Make sure the cook hears; it is a sign of approval.

A NOTE FROM THE AUTHOR

I first published most of these stories on my blog, *The Tranquilo Traveler*, where they still reside—in their original, raw-blogged, unedited glory. Go to www.JoshuaBerman.net and click on "Honeymoon" to see more.

ACKNOWLEDGMENTS

Thank you to American Jewish World Service, a world-class, worldwide development organization and "community of Jewish global citizens fighting for a better world." By offering grants and assistance to local advocates around the world, they strive to give a voice to the most oppressed, neglected, and persecuted populations. Please support them and get involved: www.ajws.org.

To all our many hosts, guides, companions, friends, translators, and fellow travelers who shared the experience with us, thank you from the bottom of our hearts. We hope to see you all again some day, somewhere. We have a special thank you for Sarmishtha Biswas, Debasish Chokraborty, Bulbulda, Sabah, Effo, Yaya, Aseye, Baba, Fatou, Little Sutay, Emily Paul, and the Wainstains.

Thank you to my editorial dream team! Jody Berman of Berman Editorial (no relation, just good luck); Timm Bryson for the covers and design; Ann Erwin for additional copyediting and proofreading. Thank you to Scott Lussier of Passport Maps for designing the five maps that appear in *Crocodile Love*.

Scott's company, PassportMaps.com, allows you to create your own custom, printable route maps that tell the story of your travels.

After years of toiling on this project between babies and diaper changes, I went to my friends and family via Kickstarter. To my backers, from the bottom of my travelin' shoes, thank you for believing in me and in this book:

Renée Alexander, Brad Allgood, Beth Berman, Steven Berman, Richard T. Berman, Todd Berman, Cheryann Beruldsen, Scott Blakeman, Rich Bradfield, Connie Boyle, Benjamin Chait, Gary M. Chandler, Jeff Christiansen, Callie Elizabeth Clark, Douglas Cushnie, Joan Daniels, Louise Daniels, Derek & Jamie Deutsch, Brian Deutsch, David Deutsch, Helen Deutsch, Daryle Dickens, Johnny Dunbar, Janet Duncan, Judy Farber, Conor Farley, Matt Faust, Ellen First, Cara Forster, Ze Frank, Caroline Gaines, Pat Gallaway, Melissa Gaskill, Sean Gaughan, Marianne Gellar, Michael Gerba, Betsy Gilliland, Lebawit Lily Girma, Cindy Glassgold, Assaf Gordon, Carol Gould, Deborah Gulperin, Cynthia Harwood, Phoebe Haupt, Shawna Kaplan Hausman, Jeanne Hedden, Carolyn B. Heller, Latane Hill, Andrew Hyde, Radhanatha Jakupko, Dan Jantzen, Deb Cole Kelner, Adam Klein, Neil Kogut, Kitty Kogut, Ryan Lamberg, Beth Leuchten, Carol Levack, Jan Linsley, Bonnie Lipton, Laura Martone, Sharon Matthews, Hugh McDonald, Jeff McLucas, Nicholas Melillo, Andrew Middleton, David Milikow, Amy Murin, Ed & Anne O'Donnell, Synnova O'Gorman, Laura Osofsky, Joshua Packman, Zev Paiss, Tom Pamperin, Angela Parham, Emily Paul, Robert Pittman, Matt Price, Charles Purshouse, Amy Robertson, Tom Romano, Anne Ross, Brendan Ross, Craig Rubens, Donald Samson, Trudy Savage, Amy Scott, Sheri

Sebilian, Helen Siegler, Freida Schiff, Jessica Schugel, Nina Sokol, Janice Soucy, Josh Spector, Peter Speek, Alan Swart, Dave Taylor, James Thompson, John Thullen, Kelsey Timmerman, Benjamin Wainstain, Claire Walter, Joel Warner, Patrick Weiland, Barry S. Weisner, Cedar Spring Wolf, Josh Wolff, and Joyce Zimmer.

Joshua Berman is a travel writer and Spanish teacher based in Boulder, Colorado. He writes a monthly column for *The Denver Post* called "Around Colorado" and is the author of five guidebooks with Avalon Travel Publishing: *Moon Nicaragua, Moon Belize, Living Abroad in Nicaragua, Maya 2012,* and *Colorado Camping. Crocodile Love* is his first narrative travel book. His website is www.JoshuaBerman.net.